EAST ANGLIA
at
WAR
═══1939-1945═══

Derek E. Johnson

JARROLD

Other titles by the same author:
Of Dogs & Duty
Leisure in Essex
War Medals
Collecting Militaria
Essex Curiosities
Collector's Guide to Militaria
East Anglia at War ... 1939-1945 (first edition)
Victorian Shooting Days
East Anglian Sporting Days
East Anglia & the Great War in Old Pictures
Exodus of Children

EAST ANGLIA AT WAR
Designed and produced by Parke Sutton Publishing Limited, Norwich
for Jarrold Publishing, Norwich.

Editor: Jan Orchard   Designer: Gillian Matthews

This edition first published 1992
Text copyright © 1992 Derek E Johnson

ISBN 0-7117-0598-4

Printed in Great Britain

CONTENTS

FOREWORD 5

CHAPTER ONE *Talk of War* 7-14

CHAPTER TWO *Save the Children* 15-24

CHAPTER THREE *Defending the Homeland* 25-40

CHAPTER FOUR *Civilians at War* 41-48

CHAPTER FIVE *Down on the Farm* 49-52

CHAPTER SIX *Industry at War* 53-60

CHAPTER SEVEN *The War at Sea* 61-72

CHAPTER EIGHT *Death from the Air* 73-98

CHAPTER NINE *The Brylcreem Boys* 99-104

CHAPTER TEN *The Yanks are Coming* 105-116

CHAPTER ELEVEN *The Road to Victory* 117-124

CHAPTER TWELVE *Mysteries and Secrets* 125-140

CHAPTER THIRTEEN *On the Home Front* 141-148

CHAPTER FOURTEEN *Glossary* 149-175

ACKNOWLEDGMENTS *176*

WAR DEAD AT CANNOCK CHASE

'And the moaning on the wind
shall be the mourning of their hearts –
and the rain from every cloud
their tears eternal.'

Victor S. Wilson

FOREWORD

Although East Anglia today includes Northamptonshire, Lincolnshire and Bedfordshire, I have restricted this second edition of *East Anglia at War* to the heartland of Essex, Suffolk, Norfolk and Cambridgeshire.

East Anglia played a vital part in the defence of Great Britain throughout the war. Radar was born here on the Suffolk coast; secret weapons testing ranges around the Rendlesham Forest and Sudbourne Marsh areas are still cloaked beneath an all-powerful security blanket, and what happened at Shingle Street will, perhaps, always remain a mystery.

Roadblocks, pillboxes and vast tank traps were thrown up around the area in a desperate bid to repel invasion. Fortunately, these steel and concrete strongholds were never put to the test, but even today you can still catch a glimpse of a lone pillbox or dragon's tooth tank trap tucked away by the side of a country railway track or by an isolated river bank ... grim reminders of those early war years.

There were 109 strategic airbases scattered across East Anglia, playing host to flyers from many nations. Canadians, Australians, Poles, Czechs, New Zealanders, South Africans, British and American forces operated from these bases. During its three year stay in the region, the American Eighth Airforce suffered 46,456 casualties.

This, the second and revised edition of *East Anglia at War* is the moving story of how the region fared. In the 1914-18 war, East Anglia suffered its fair share of enemy action in the form of long distance shelling and Zeppelin and Gotha bombing raids. In 1939, no-one knew for sure what to expect once war was declared. In the end, there were no winners or losers. Nearly every family lost someone in the six years of conflict. The war brought drastic changes to the region as old standards and values vanished overnight and families found themselves split up, sometimes for good.

Derek E Johnson

CHAPTER ONE

Talk of War

*W*hen Britain eventually declared war on Germany that fateful day in September 1939, it came as no great surprise to the people of East Anglia. Many had already been involved in civil defence exercises as preparation for a conflict most saw as inevitable.

As early as 1938, Whitehall pundits had been trying to arouse public interest – with limited success – in ARP, Civil Defence and the Red Cross. A special effort was made in East Anglia, as the authorities realised just how vulnerable this isolated region was.

In 1937, the Committee of Imperial Defence decided that the only civilian installations in the area worth the cost of defending were the American Oil Company, based at Ipswich, Norwich power station and the oil depot at King's Lynn. Two factions were involved in the defence project; those who could see the sense of establishing an adequate line of defence across East Anglia, and those who controlled the finances. The final outcome resulted in the 1st AA Division, detailed to defend the south of the region, being poorly equipped with just 120 searchlights and outdated first world war naval guns, completely unsuitable for anti-aircraft use.

Manning the guns presented another major problem as the government couldn't justify the expense of training and equipping regular troops. A grand scheme was hatched, involving local workers aged between 35 and 55. Called the National Defence Battery, these men were supposed to defend their factories with the poor equipment available. The purse strings were loosened sufficiently to increase production of the Bofors light AA gun, but it is recorded that public opposition to the siting of AA batteries around the region meant that many of the defence plans were shelved.

Those public spirited stalwarts who always seem to be at the forefront in times of national crisis had started serious training during the autumn and winter of 1938. In Colchester, 80,000 volunteers were recruited. Most were from the older generation. Their task should war break out was to identify poison gas, administer first aid, organise rescue and medical services and shepherd people to the safety of public air raid shelters.

The almost non-existent defences of many East Anglian towns were further weakened when important equipment was despatched to less vulnerable locations. As early as autumn 1935, a steady erosion of resources had been introduced when equipment was shipped to the Malta garrison as there were fears of war with Italy when Mussolini invaded Abyssinia.

Practical knowledge of the type of bombs and missiles likely to be used by the enemy was sketchy and ill-informed. Apart from the rather primitive fire bombs and missiles dropped by Zeppelin and Gotha bombers during the first world war, even the authorities were at a complete loss as to what to expect.

Newspapers and magazines ran features on how best to protect yourself in an air raid. W D & H O Wills brought out a series of Air Raid Precautions cigarette cards, complete with details on how to construct a refuge room, mask windows, strip down and service a gas mask, tackle incendiary bombs and other hazards.

ARP units in East Anglia could be seen training at weekends, tackling incendiary bombs with a long handled shovel, a dustbin lid and buckets of sand and earth. In rural parts of Norfolk, Suffolk and Essex, a coal shovel mounted on the handle end of a pitchfork served a double purpose as the fork end could be used to drag off burning thatch.

The annual Home Defence Exercise in which East Anglia played an important part saw aircraft, AA and searchlight batteries working in conjunction using limited resources. During those early days, East Anglia boasted about 20 searchlight companies, manning 60 searchlights. Each site accommodated 16 men who took it in turn to man the sound locators, generator and light.

Early in 1939, every household was issued with the National Service Handbook, detailing what people could do to help in the crisis. Fit men up to the age of 50 could join reserve and demolition parties and decontamination squads. Men between 30 and 50, and women between 18 and 50 could join the ambulance service. Women over 18 and men over 45 would be employed as clerks, doorkeepers, switchboard operators or stenographers in report centres. Those under 18 were to be part of a communications service, acting as messengers by bike, motor bike or on foot.

The summer saw the start of black-out precautions. This was a lesson painfully learned in the last war, when Zeppelin and Gotha bombers had flown in over the East Anglian coastline using the lights from shops and cottages as a guide. One enemy raider had homed in on his Norfolk target using the glowing firebox of a train as his beacon.

In the early days of the war, blacking-out meant pinning material over the window using thumb tacks or large headed felt nails. When it was realised the war wouldn't be 'all over by Christmas,' the material was fixed to wooden frames which could be lifted into place. The alternative to black fabric was a set of heavy folding shutters around each window. One Norwich lady painted the inside of her shutters with a country scene. "I wanted to be like John Constable." she explained.

Gas masks were issued – it was seriously believed that the enemy would use poison gas. The tops of GPO letter boxes were coated with yellow gas detector paint, and decontamination squads could be seen practising on glum, often unwilling, volunteers. Car owners were shown how to immobilise their vehicles – failure to do this meant a heavy fine. Bus stations were under guard to stop the enemy commandeering vehicles.

The Government kept some of its preparations secret from the public. Food was stockpiled in underground dumps scattered about the country, and fold-away cardboard coffins were issued to local authorities. Certain buildings, usually well away from the town centre, were selected as mortuaries.

All sorts of regulations were introduced. Homes could be searched without prior warning and for all sorts of reasons, including storing more than a week's supply of food, or for failing to extinguish lights when ordered. In an emergency, a householder could be forced to move out. Refusing to take in strangers when ordered to by a billeting officer meant a £50 fine.

Anyone carrying a camera came under close scrutiny. The sounding of hooters, bells, whistles or any other sort of noise maker was forbidden.

Those from the great open spaces of East Anglia found the law forbidding the flying of model aircraft particularly hard to bear. In 1939, the Daily Sketch carried a story of spies being captured on the east coast while transmitting coded messages to the enemy, using a kite fitted with an automatic signalling device. It was hard too for the region's many boat owners. Amateur yachtsmen who failed to remove their craft from the water suffered the hardship of having the boat sent to a watery grave by a series of axe blows delivered beneath the water line. The official view was that invaders could use small craft to ferry supplies across waterways.

With the passing of the Emergency Powers (Defence) Bill, aliens suddenly found themselves classified as enemies. Italians, Germans, Austrians and those of obscure and suspicious Slav origin were rounded up and sent to camps around the country. Once at the camp, a tribunal decided whether the alien was A class (instant internment), B class (restricted movement or C class (allowed free). Those unfortunate enough to be A class were housed in

Olympia in London, then moved to Butlins at Clacton and Warners in Dovercourt. At Clacton, the camp was organised and run by the inmates, with a full-blooded Nazi baron elected as leader. He is best remembered for the noisy 'smoker' concerts held to entertain fellow internees, at which he would loudly and proudly sing a selection of Nazi war songs.

Once war had been declared, the population imagined there would be instant action. Instead, a strange period of inactivity, which became known as the 'Phoney War,' followed, stretching from September 1939 to May 1940. Extracts from the official War Diary recall these early days.

Monday, 4 September, 1939
Observations by the RAF indicated that the black-out was generally effective. There were, however, exceptions, and steps have been taken to inform the responsible authorities in any town where lights were clearly visible. No reports of enemy action have been received today. Evacuation has continued smoothly, although there have been local difficulties. The completion of preparatory measures is still in progress. Difficulties in staffing Report and Control centres have been experienced, particularly in Norfolk, West Suffolk and the Isle of Ely.

Wednesday, 6th September
Enemy aircraft was stated to have been observed over the south-eastern part of Waltham Holy Cross in Essex (in fact, there were no enemy aircraft involved in this action in which Fighter Command suffered its first casualty).

Saturday, 9th September
Cambridge reports that the important March railway marshalling yard, the largest in Europe, is illuminated by level crossing lamps. There is great discontent and concern among the railway staff and local residents.

Tuesday, 12th September
The general position of ARP services in the Cambridge region is reported satisfactory, but there are certain deficiencies in Ipswich and Norfolk. At Ipswich, ambulance first aid parties and repair squads are under strength and there is a serious lack of co-ordination in Norfolk.

Wednesday, 13th September
Southend and Tilbury sirens sounded for two minutes at 1345 hours as a result of a short circuit. In reply to an inquiry, Regions were instructed that rescue, stretcher and ambulance parties and fire services should fulfil their duties while a raid is in progress. In view of some uncertainty in the matter, the Chief Rabbi has asked that Jewish air raid wardens should not absent themselves from duty on Jewish festivals, except to attend services when that can be arranged.

Thursday, 21st September

It is reported via the Cabinet War Room that the floodlighting of the Butlin's and Dovercourt internment camps is still exciting alarm and indignation among local inhabitants.

Sunday, 8th October

Reconnaissance in Cambridge and West Norfolk revealed that many lights were visible in buildings in King's Lynn and Wisbech. Car lights and railway lights in this area were also visible. The black-out was generally effective in the neighbourhood of Cambridge, but car lights made roads visible.

Tuesday, 24th October

No enemy action has been reported during this period. Sixteen Greek seamen from the crew of the steamer *Konstantinos Hadyipateros*, sunk by enemy action, were rescued and landed at Great Yarmouth uninjured.

Saturday, 4th November

Changes in the regulations governing the hours of black-out and the closing time of places of entertainment were broadcast to the Regions. A mine washed up on November 2nd at Aldeburgh (some ten miles north of Withersea) exploded, causing damage to the windows of some 25 bungalows. No casualties were reported.

PRACTISE PUTTING ON YOUR RESPIRATOR

1. Hold your breath. (*To inhale gas may be fatal.*) 2. Hold mask in front of face, thumbs inside straps. 3. Thrust chin well forward into mask. Pull straps as far over head as they will go. 4. Run finger round face-piece taking care head-straps are not twisted.

MAKE SURE IT FITS

See that the rubber fits snugly at sides of jaw and under chin. The head-straps should be adjusted so that they hold the mask firmly on the face. To test for fit, hold a piece of soft, flat rubber or of soft tissue paper to end of mask and breathe in. The rubber or paper should stick.

Arrows indicate points needing particular attention

YOUR RESPIRATOR

COMPLETELY PROTECTS YOUR EYES, NOSE, THROAT AND LUNGS AGAINST ALL WAR GASES

ALWAYS KEEP YOUR RESPIRATOR SAFE, CLEAN AND EFFICIENT

IF YOU SUSPECT GAS, AT ONCE PUT ON YOUR RESPIRATOR AND GET UNDER COVER

7/40. (1167/1327.) Wt. 1633. 200M. 8/42. A., P. & S., Ltd. 428.   34—9999

Saturday, 18th November

... *HMS Ganges* (Shotley) sounded an air raid warning at Harwich at 1140 hours. The public were warned to take shelter. Raiders Passed was given a few minutes later.

Monday, 20th November
Yellow warnings were issued to the Chelmsford and North London areas between 1219 and 1242 hours when an unidentified plane was seen flying east over Thurrock, Essex. It was fired on by AA and there was slight damage to roofs from shell splinters.

Thursday, 30th November
A barrage balloon which grounded at 0010 hours at Rainham railway station interrupted traffic on both lines and caused some damage to signals and telegraph wires. Another balloon is reported grounded at Little Bardfield (five miles east of Thaxted).

Wednesday, 6th December
The presence of enemy or unidentified aircraft over the Midlands and off the east coast gave rise to a number of yellow warnings this morning. 3/Kunstenfliegergruppe 506 (Heinkel 115-2081) flew into radio mast at West Beckham Chain Home station and crashed on to west beach, Sheringham, Norfolk at 3.15 am. Aircraft S4+Bl wrecked. Three crew members killed.

Friday, 8th December
East Suffolk police report that unidentified aircraft were in the neighbourhood of Felixstowe and Orfordness between 2155 and 2237 hours on 7.12.39. An aeroplane, presumed hostile, was also in the neighbourhood of Orford lighthouse at 0015 hours on 8.12.39.

Monday, 11th December
No enemy action has been reported during this period. A Blenheim fighter from Debden (Essex) crashed in Great Chesterford Park at 0030 hours today. The pilot, Flt Lt William Packer, was killed and the gunner, LAC Edwin Jones injured.

Tuesday, 12th December
No enemy action has been reported during this period. Five survivors of the collier *Marwick Head* have been landed at Yarmouth today, and 33 of the motor vessel *King Egbert*.

Wednesday, 20th December
The Chief Constable of East Essex reports that mines were washed ashore today at Sizewell Gap and Aldeburgh.

Tuesday, 26th December
No enemy action has been reported during this period. The Essex police report that a white canvas balloon (conical shaped and about the size of two

footballs) was picked up on the beach at Holland-on-Sea near Clacton at 1730 hours, December 25th. This has not, at present, been identified.

During that first winter of the war, the public, not surprisingly, honestly thought that they had been hoodwinked by the authorities. Where was the action, the raids, the excitement? All they had experienced so far was a series of irksome restrictions and red tape. Black-out procedure became lax in some areas, and many evacuees returned home to Mum and Dad.

ARP and Civil Defence training continued – but it was dull work, as these extracts from a diary kept by the late Mr A B Kennell of Holland-on-Sea illustrate.

18th January, 1940
Attended lecture about incendiary bombs.

24th.....
Whist drive held in aid of soldiers. £2 raised.

30th.....
A mine was washed up at the sluice gates and blew up. It made an awful noise. Two others were washed up near Clacton - no harm done. I found a piece of the mine 500 yards away on the cliffs.

1st February
Issued with ARP uniform.

8th.....
At 10.15 am, a mine blew a big hole in the middle of the pier. It shattered hundreds of windows.

26th.....
A busy day. First took straw and clinker up to bombing ground, then watched Woolworths and Marks and Spencer girls go through their practice. They did very well too.

1st March
Clean up lorry for our county exercises on Sunday. ARP party tonight but did not go.

11th.....
Squad started drilling at St Mary's Hall. Have got some repair jobs at the place, a brick wall to build. Had practice turn out at night. Quite an exciting day. Gradually getting my ARP uniform together.

Things weren't so quiet at sea. Magnetic mines were proving a major hazard. On the outbreak of war, the entire British minesweeping fleet was equipped to handle contact mines as no one thought a magnetic mine would be used. Between September and October 1939, 59,027 tons of shipping were sent to the bottom by mines. On November 21, the destroyer *Gipsy* fell foul of a mine off Harwich, with the loss of 30 lives.

Dieses Haus darf nur mit Genehmigung des Befehlshabers der Sicherheitspolizei für Grossbritannien betreten werden.

No entrance without permission of the Chief-in Command of the German Secret Police for Great Britain.

German confidence that invasion was imminent is obvious from the notice printed above - one of thousands prepared by the Nazi High Command.

CHAPTER TWO

Save the Children

*I*n those early days of the war, the situation looked truly grim. No one knew what might happen, or when bombing might start. The Government honestly believed that strafing and bombing raids would demoralise the public to the extent that mass panic would set in, causing roads, canals and the railways to become blocked with frightened refugees. This had already happened in Europe, and the authorities were determined that chaos and confusion would not be allowed to set in here.

As a result, it was decided to begin mass evacuation of children, moving them away from likely danger zones to the country or the seaside. At first, it was felt that evacuation plans should be left to individual local authorities, but as some counties were less civil defence minded than others, it soon became obvious that this approach would not work.

Because evacuation plans appeared to be chronically disorganised at the beginning of 1939, the Ministry of Health found itself faced with two tasks. Short range measures were needed in case the situation deteriorated suddenly. While these plans were being thought out, it was also necessary to prepare a more complex, detailed plan for the evacuation of around 4,000,000 persons.

Priority classes were drawn up, ready for the mass move.

Class 1: School children removed as school units under the charge of their teachers.

Class 2: Younger children accompanied by mother or some other responsible person.

Class 3: Expectant mothers.

Class 4: Adult blind persons and cripples whose removal was feasible.

It had already been decided that evacuees would be billeted in private homes. This was not a popular idea, and a number of MPs representing rural areas of East Anglia petitioned the Minister of Health to think seriously of building large camps instead. One county council feared that householders would end up taking in 'the dregs of London'.

Although such an attitude seems selfish now, one must remember that back in the late 1930s , the majority of East Anglian country folk were set in their ways, didn't take kindly to changes and believed that strangers usually brought trouble.

Undaunted, the authorities went ahead with their plans, and on Friday September 1, two days after children were evacuated from Paris, the great move started.

Rallied behind an impressive array of banners and flags, sporting armbands, tickets and labels, groups of children waited patiently for their trains. Unfortunately, train timetables had not been adequately prepared in advance, and groups were herded into the nearest available railway carriage. Individual schools were divided, classes scattered and families split up and sent to towns and villages miles apart. In one instance, a group of children split from their main school party found themselves dumped at a tiny Norfolk railway halt, miles from anywhere. A kindly farmer took them in. Some six months later, the authorities managed to track down their lost charges only to find they had become part and parcel of the farmer's work force.

Newspapers carried stirring tales of the evacuation. This extract is from the Essex County Standard, September 2, 1939.

'*14,000 evacuees from London to the outside of Colchester were begun on Friday 1st. Areas chiefly affected being those under the Lexden, Winstree and Tendring Rural District Councils which will each receive 5,500 evacuees. Brightlingsea Council will deal with 1,600 persons, Wivenhoe with 500 and West Mersea with 900. Arriving in batches of 4,000 per day, it is estimated that there will be four train loads in each of the first three days and two on the Monday.*

Each child is being issued with 48 hours emergency ration, Helpers include teachers, Boy Scouts and Girl Guides. The general public are requested not to congregate at railway stations so as not to hinder the work of the officials ....'

Childhood memories of evacuation vary. Some recall a time of utter confusion with just one or two memorable highlights. Others remember every detail.

For Hazel Gutteridge, the most outstanding memory was witnessing the evacuation of the circus from Clacton Pier. She recalls seeing two elephants standing near the railings in the car park being fed with chunks of bread. One, in mischievous mood, snatched up a towel which had been hung on the railings to dry, and with a defiant toss of its head, threw it down into the sea. Everyone laughed, breaking the sad atmosphere.

Hazel also recalls being vaccinated, suffering seemingly endless medical examinations and being measured for a gas mask. Amidst floods of tears, all inflammable toys, including the then-popular celluloid dolls were burnt in the back garden as it was felt they would add fuel to fires caused by bombing.

Evacuees were moved by train, bus and paddle steamer. The move was particularly urgent in areas such as Dagenham, where heavy industry would be a priority target for the enemy. In four days, 17,000 children and teachers were moved by water from the Dagenham area – as their Evacuation Officer J G O'Leary recalls.

"August 31st was a lovely day, and the boats of the Central Steam Navigation Co moved out into a golden, early morning mist. The boats were so quiet - no singing, not a cheer. Otherwise, all was in good order. All we knew was that they would reach Felixstowe, Yarmouth and Lowestoft in the course of the day. We knew that from these places, parties would be moved out into the Norfolk and East Suffolk countryside. When the boats arrived, the authorities were aghast at the numbers. There wasn't any organisation to deal with them. Schools and other buildings were opened, but bedding and blankets did not exist. In some cases, teachers, mothers and children lived on apples, milk and cheese for four days. They slept on straw, covered by grain bags."

Elsie De Negri, now Elsie Blackborn, was evacuated from Dagenham, and recalls the days of waiting to hear when the evacuation would begin. At the time, Elsie was a 10 year old schoolgirl. Her most vivid memory is of the family being discriminated against by tradesmen because they had a foreign name – even though both her mother and father were Dagenham born and bred – an attitude typical of the times.

"Nobody could be sure when the evacuation would be, and I remember we had to take a little pack of sandwiches to school every day, just in case. I was always scared that today would be the day I would have to go. When I did go, I was split up from most of my brothers and sisters. We were sent to different places, depending on the school we went to. I went to a farmer and his wife in Somerset. They were very nice, but I was frightened at having to leave my Mum. After about 11 months, I went home. I couldn't stand being away, it was making me ill. Gradually, most of the other children came home and schooling started again. We had some good times."

Many of the children treated evacuation as a great adventure and weren't at all worried about leaving Mum and Dad – as a former pupil of Wanstead County High School recalls.

"We all gathered in the school grounds with other children from Wanstead and Woodford, then boarded double-deckers. It was the first time I had been away from my parents, but I don't recall any feeling of fright, only excitement. The bus went to Chelmsford bus station. Very kind ladies had buckets of lemonade and biscuits ready for us. My friends and myself on the upper deck took great delight in continually asking for more drinks only to tip them out of the window on the far side."

The inactivity of the Phoney War didn't encourage the evacuees to stay put and, much to the consternation of the Government, many started to drift home. Used to the bright lights, most of them hated the cold, wet, boring countryside. Relationships between townies and country folk became strained, trouble of various sorts broke out, and the Government announced that it was prepared to compensate householders for any damage to property caused by evacuees.

Evacuation troubles in West Mersea were highlighted in a report dated September 16.

'After nearly a fortnight of acute tension in the district, things are beginning to settle down. Some 30 families who were unable to find solace away from their own districts, and some half dozen children have been taken back. Quite naturally, many adjustments will have to be made, but sympathy will go out to those who have unaccompanied children, for here, in many cases, they are refusing to accept their new conditions, and to add to this, many parents have visited their children several times and left behind a state which it baffles the kindest of folk to rectify.'

The migration of returning children was only brought to a halt by events in Europe. As German forces occupied country after country, the defenders found themselves pushed back in full retreat. Members of the BEF awaited rescue on the French beaches ... invasion was a real possibility.

But, if invasion came, it would come to the coast – where many children had been sent for safety. During spring and early summer of 1940, yet another phase of the evacuation operation took place as children, expectant mothers, the disabled and handicapped were moved from East Anglian and south coast resorts. May 19–23, 1940 saw 5500 children transferred to South Wales. On June 2, a further 6650 were evacuated and in the following weeks, 25,000 youngsters were moved from a ten mile zone along the coasts of Suffolk, Norfolk, Essex, Sussex and Kent. All state schools in the danger zone were evacuated. By autumn 1940, about 49,500 unaccompanied children and 56,000 children and adults from coastal areas had been moved to reception centres. Within the next eight months, a further 328,000 left the dangerous coastal area for safer regions further inland.

Such mass movement caused problems for parents, children and the authorities. A schoolmaster recalls the re-evacuation of children from the Frinton/Walton region.

"We left Walton at 1.05 am, stopped at Colchester, Ipswich and Cambridge. We had any amount of water to drink, and the WVS and railway people were very helpful. We arrived at Stroud at 7.50 pm. The children were wonderful – never a complaint or grumble."

For Beryl Walter, a schoolgirl living with her family on the east coast, the outbreak of war held many horrors.

"Tension was, perhaps, a little heightened at home, as we avidly listened to every news bulletin, but we continued daily life. The routine of school work was comforting too. As the days progressed, there were changes. Troops moved in and dug trenches, complete with terrifyingly large guns covered in branches for camouflage. Those first few months passed uneventfully, although gas masks, which we carried at all times, together with our new identity cards were a constant reminder of the threat."

"One night in April, I woke, trembling, as explosions echoed through the night. I wanted to call out, but no sound would come. What a relief it was to hear my mother's voice. I dashed into her room. My brother and sister were there in bed, snuggled together for warmth, but shivering with fear, waiting for what was to happen next. Had the action really started ? Was this the war ? Gradually, dawn came and with it release of tension with talk and cups of tea."

"It seemed hard to go to school that morning, uncertain what the day might bring. Once there, we found most of the windows broken, but lessons went on as usual. We were forbidden to go near the devastated area, which was cordoned off and guarded. It was a great attraction for souvenir hunters."

The authorities realised that bombing in these coastal areas could bring about massive casualties. Mass evacuation of children like Beryl was vital.

"On Sunday night, I was already in bed when my sister came in crying. She had just heard on the nine o'clock news that we were to be evacuated. The next three days blurred into tears, preparations and farewells, to pets as well as people."

"Early on the Thursday morning, we gathered at the railway station with our parents, not knowing when, or if, we would ever see each other again. Our destination was secret, we had labels around our necks, carried very little luggage and had a packet of sandwiches. The journey, in a grubby train, seemed endless. Teachers walked the corridors, seeing that all was well. They gave us sweets and drinks, but couldn't do anything for our aching hearts or our loneliness. We eventually arrived in the Midlands, eight hours later."

Norah Hodgkinson, evacuated from Dovercourt to North Nibley in Gloucestershire remembers the journey as a big adventure. Most vivid of all was the journey through the Ipswich railway tunnel, during which playful friends dared her to get up and prod their accompanying middle-aged teacher Miss Cross in the childish hope that she would shriek with fright in the dark.

One of Norah's main concerns was the loss of a bag of barley sugar sweets packed by Mum for the journey. She also took childish delight in hearing that many of the big boys, seen stuffing themselves with chocolate and oranges on Dovercourt station had come to grief.

Nearer their destination, a number of children were overcome by heat and travel sickness. "Two of them I particularly pitied", Norah remembers. "One was sick right into the open hood hanging down the back of the other's coat. I bore up well until the next day, when my foster family's dog retrieved my morning porridge."

It was fondly imagined by both parents and the authorities that the children would be safe and well cared for in their new homes. In reality, many were allowed to run wild. Several were drowned playing around the numerous emergency fire service tanks erected in open ground. These were later covered to deter children. Town children sent to rural districts fell victim to the temptation of playing around waterways, often with tragic consequences. Saddest of all was the fate of young Norman Shaw, evacuated from Suffolk to Wansop, Nottingham, and killed in a bombing raid during an outing to Sheffield.

There were unscrupulous foster parents who saw evacuees as a way of making money by cramming as many as possible into homes and outhouses. Some children from respectable, middle class homes found themselves sent to cramped country cottages with outside earth closets – a real worry for townies, afraid to venture down the garden path in the dark. It isn't surprising that many of them were bed wetters!

One little girl, evacuated from Great Yarmouth with her brother was sent to Keyworth, Nottingham. Taken into a small schoolroom, and plied with refreshments, she recalls "being looked over like sheep in a cattle market. People wanted a boy, a girl or two of the same. Nobody seemed to want one of each sex. Soon all the other children had been chosen, leaving me and my brother alone."

Daisy Cannell, also from Great Yarmouth recalls evacuation with mixed feelings. She and her sisters were sent to Kinoulton near Nottingham. Once again, the children were herded into a local school to be looked over.

"Perhaps being an older child among the young ones made me feel ill at ease, for I certainly didn't like the way I could hear people discussing who they would take and why. Looking back, I realise it was all kindly meant and that all sorts of things had to be taken into consideration. Our parents didn't want us to be split up, and eventually, we were the only three left in the classroom. It was awful, sitting there while they discussed what to do with

The end of the war meant reunion with Mum – and victory street parties for Britain's children.

A group of youngsters, awaiting evacuation at Colchester station, being shown the workings of a service rifle by James Turner of the Royal Artillery.

us. Eventually, they decided to send us to a Mrs White who had said she could take one or two evacuees if no other place could be found, but the arrangement would be temporary."

Happily, the sisters' dread of being parted went unfounded and they stayed together.

Not all children were as lucky. Two little Essex girls nearly starved to death. Billeted in a cottage with a fearsome old lady, they were subjected to a reign of terror – as one of them recalls.

"When we arrived after a very long journey, all the old dear had for us was a plate of cold mutton, mint sauce and dry bread. We refused to eat the mutton, making the excuse that we didn't eat meat. We made do with the dried bread and mint sauce. From that day on, for all the time we were there, we never saw another piece of fresh meat. On Sundays, if we were lucky, we had corned beef or tinned pilchards. This was supposed to be a great secret and the old lady warned us that if we told anyone she would turn us into frogs. We believed her – we were only young. Even when the school health inspectors called to find out why we looked so undernourished, we didn't dare say anything. We really did think she was a witch."

"About once a month, our parents used to send a large parcel in answer to our frantic cries for food. We were allowed to open the first parcel and keep the contents, but once the old dear saw what had been sent, we were never allowed to keep another parcel. She used to send them to her daughter in Birmingham. On another occasion, after I had pestered my father for a bicycle, a scooter arrived as bikes were not to be had for love nor money. I managed a couple of scoots up and down the garden path before she wrapped the scooter up and sent it off to her daughter."

Ever since the beginning of the war, some wealthy families had sent their children to safety in the USA, Canada, Australia and New Zealand. The day that France capitulated to the Germans, the Government decided that this scheme should be extended to those who couldn't afford to pay. Not everyone agreed – Winston Churchill remarked in a minute to the Home Secretary Sir John Anderson:

'*I certainly do not propose to send a message by the senior child to Mr Mackenzie King*' (then Prime Minister of Canada), '*or by the junior child either. If I sent a message by anyone, it would be that I entirely deprecate any stampede from this country at the present time.*'

Despite these caustic observations, the Children's Overseas Reception Board was set up under the control of Geoffrey Shakespeare, Parliamentary Secretary of the Dominions Office. Once the Board had been established, it soon became apparent that large numbers wanted to escape to safety. When it was finally announced that no further requests could be handled, 21,000

applications for children aged between five and sixteen years had been received by the Board.

Those shipped overseas under the Children's Overseas Reception Board scheme became known as CORB's. One former CORB who sailed for Australia aboard the Polish liner *Batory* was Philip Stone from Mistley in Essex. Aged nine, he travelled with his brothers Michael, 12 and Geoffrey, 14, and regarded the whole thing as a huge adventure. Philip recalls having to be called to kiss his mother goodbye, such was the excitement.

Once aboard, the brothers soon became used to carrying lifebelts and to wearing metal discs bearing their identity numbers. Over half a century later, all three remember those numbers – 493,494 and 495.

Sadly, this great exodus of children to safety overseas could not continue. The writing must have been on the wall when the Dutch liner, *SS Volendam*, carrying 335 evacuees to New York via Halifax was damaged by torpedoes in mid-Atlantic on Friday, August 30, 1940. Fortunately, the children were rescued and landed in Scotland a few days later. On September 17, the *City of Benares* carrying 197 passengers and 209 crew was sunk in mid-Atlantic with terrible loss of life, and the Government decided it was no longer safe to ship large numbers of children overseas, although evacuation did continue in small numbers.

Many of those shipped to foreign parts never returned to East Anglia, but built new lives in their adopted countries.

IMPORTANT NOTICE

To the inhabitants of certain towns in Defence Areas who have received instructions to be ready to leave the towns at short notice.

This leaflet is being distributed throughout the country. You will want to know how it affects you, in view of the instructions you have received to be ready to leave the town at short notice.

When evacuation from the town is ordered you will receive definite instructions from the Police. If, for any reason, you receive no order for evacuation from the Police, or if the order is cancelled, you must obey the instructions contained in this leaflet and STAY WHERE YOU ARE.

Issued by the Ministry of   *Information on behalf of the War Office and the Ministry of Home Security*

STAY WHERE YOU ARE

IF this island is invaded by sea or air everyone who is not under orders must stay where he or she is. This is not simply advice : it is an order from the Government, and you must obey it just as soldiers obey their orders. Your order is " Stay Put," **but remember that this does not apply until invasion comes.**

WHY MUST I STAY PUT?

Because in France, Holland and Belgium, the Germans were helped by the people who took flight before them. Great crowds of refugees blocked all roads. The soldiers who could have defended them could not get at the enemy. The enemy used the refugees as a human shield. These refugees were got out on to the roads by rumour and false orders. Do not be caught out in this way. Do not take any notice of any story telling what the enemy has done or where he is. Do not take orders except from the Military, the Police, the Home Guard (L.D.V.) and the A.R.P. authorities or wardens.

WHAT WILL HAPPEN TO ME IF I DON'T STAY PUT?

If you do not stay put you will stand a very good chance of being killed. The enemy may machine-gun you from the air in order to increase

CHAPTER THREE

Defending the Homeland

*I*n the early days of the war, Britain's position was unenviable. Invasion was a very real threat – and East Anglia, geographically close to occupied Europe was certain to be a target area.

Four days after the invasion of Holland, on the evening of August 14, an important speech was broadcast by Mr Anthony Eden, Secretary of State for War. In this, he pointed out that Europe had been overrun by German parachutists, and to prevent such a thing taking place in Britain, a new special force was being formed.

"Since the war began, the Government has received countless enquiries from all over the kingdom from men of all ages who are, for one reason or another, not at present engaged in military service and who wish to do something for the defence of their country. Well, now is your opportunity. We want a large number of such men in Great Britain who are British subjects, between the ages of 17 and 65 to come forward and offer their services .... The name of the new force which is now being raised will be the Local Defence Volunteers .... this name describes its duties in three words."

There was an immediate rush to volunteer, especially in East Anglia. By 1942, the Essex LDV was 40,000 strong.

In the early days some village volunteers became rather too military. I have been told of volunteers armed to the teeth, refusing to let even a well-known neighbour past the check point. In the end, the police had to arrest some LDV members who insisted on marching around the highways and byways challenging all and sundry with weapons ranging from rusty old muzzle-loaders to double-barrelled elephant guns. In some cases, weapons were discharged in panic. At Romford, two sentries fired at a car which failed to stop. Four of the passengers were badly wounded and the fifth killed outright. It was thought that a noisy exhaust prevented the driver of the car hearing the challenge given by the sentries.

Because of increased concern, the Secretary of War, Sir Edmund Grigg explained in Parliament the primary function of the Home Guard (the new name for the LDV) was to guard vulnerable roads and railways and to keep watch for landings by enemy paratroopers. The Home Guard would not be armed with service rifles, but with shotguns and low calibre sporting rifles.

Where to find these arms was a problem. A nationwide appeal went out, and many old and valuable weapons were given by museums and collections around East Anglia. Many of these were muzzle-loaders, and the chance of finding proper size balls, powder, flint and percussion caps was slim. Enterprising members of the Home Guard improvised with all sorts of volatile mixtures. One commander at Gestingthorpe blew himself and five of his men to pieces while experimenting with home-made explosives. At Bury St Edmunds, an early bronze Chinese cannon was shattered into a thousand fragments when loaded with an unstable mixture. The arms situation improved later in the year when the Americans shipped over half a million first world war service rifles and bayonets.

It wasn't just members of the Home Guard who were trigger-happy. On the night of July l5, 1940 at Observer Corps post 18/J1, Woolverstone, Suffolk, the head observer, Mr J B Snell was shot in the hand and thigh by a party of over-zealous naval ratings searching for German spies. Seeing Mr Snell setting out a flare path (these were laid by the Observer Corps as a guide to returning pilots), the sailors, en route to Shotley Barracks after a good night out in Ipswich, decided he was a German agent intent on leading enemy aircraft to the naval base at Harwich and promptly opened fire!

The Home Guard were constantly on the alert for enemy parachutists in the early days of the war. For some reason, it was believed that they would arrive dressed as nuns or postmen, and there were all sorts of rumours concerning them. One of the oddest was the belief up in the Fens wildfowling country that German parachutists could only be despatched by a special bullet. This probably arose from the fact that the War Office had just issued a special ball cartridge for use against descending paratroopers.

In those early days, the Home Guard were a rag, tag and bobtail lot. For most, the only form of identification was an armband run up by the WVS. Officers tended to sport golfing, hacking or cycling outfits – although it was reported that the officers of one Essex company had turned out in all the scarlet and gold glory of the old Indian Empire.

The summer and autumn of 1940 was to see the introduction of a highly secret underground Home Guard guerilla movement; the authorities, having weighed up the situation, decided that whatever happened, once the might of the German invasion had been launched, no amount of road barricades, concealed pits filled with sharpened stakes or platoons of cutlass-swinging fanatics could ever hope to hold off a well-trained enemy for long. It was decided to form some 20 Auxiliary Units, which were to include a smattering of serving army officers and cells of Home Guard formed into guerilla bands. Their job was to take cover once the invasion came, only coming out of hiding once the bulk of the enemy had moved on, leaving a small occupation force which could be picked off.

In East Anglia, it was left to Colonel Gubbins to build a series of cells staffed by men who knew the landscape, the wind and tides, and could keep quiet. One such was Roger Weeley, known locally as the Squire of Weeley. His family were no strangers to the work of militia men, as one of his ancestors had been instrumental in raising a band of volunteers during the Napoleonic wars. His introduction to the secret army came from a childhood friend who had just returned from the evacuation of Norway.

"Telephoning me early one morning, he enquired if I would take on an important job. It required six men who knew the land and marshes from Brightlingsea to Harwich, and could keep their mouths shut. He didn't mind what sort of past criminal record they had, so long as I could trust 'em."

The Squire knew just where he could find six such likely lads, and training was soon under way.

"One evening, we had quite an interesting little exercise. Brigadier Stanyer wanted us to help test his famous Stanyer Line tank trap which was built across the back of Harwich. A lot of extra troops had been brought into the area to defend the line, and we were supposed to infiltrate through the defenders without being observed. Dressed in battle-dress overalls with faces painted black and armed with daggers, coshes, semi-automatic pistols and hand grenades, we caused quite a stir. Not only did we get through the defences unobserved, we took a fair bit of ammunition from anti-aircraft and searchlight positions. This caused a certain amount of chaos."

Security was of the utmost importance. Members did not know the identity of those in other groups in the same district. Orders were despatched covertly. The Weeley cell used a drainpipe beneath a railway bridge for their letter box. Messages posted there were picked up by an unknown person. His identity remains a secret even today.

Membership of 202 Battalion, as this secret organisation was called, asked for volunteers to live off the land and lie low wherever they could find shelter. Intricate plans were laid, so that if the invasion came, men of 202 would slip away to their hiding places to await the call to action.

These men were the first Britons to be armed with the Thompson sub-machine guns, imported from the USA; the first to have sticky bombs, the first to get the Piat anti-tank weapon; the first to have phosphorus grenades and the special tyre-bursting mine disguised as lumps of coal or horse manure. Some were given a .22 rifle, made by either BSA, Winchester or Remington and fitted with a telescopic sight and silencer. It was capable of firing high velocity bullets which could kill a man a mile away.

Rubber truncheons, Fairbairn commando daggers and thick-soled rubber boots were given to all members. Some were issued with longbows to shoot incendiary charges into German petrol dumps or pick off sentries.

Gelignite, phosphorus bombs, detonators and hand-grenades were buried around the countryside. These hideouts were the brainchild of Peter Fleming, brother of Ian, the creator of James Bond. The hideouts, known as operational bases were originally intended as places where the men could withdraw to eat, sleep or take refuge. They were scattered all around East Anglia and ranged from simple fox-holes to sophisticated brick and steel lined bunkers to accommodate six or seven men.

In an area known as Weeley Woods, Roger Weeley built a brick, concrete and steel bunker deep in the side of a small hillock. Invisible from outside, the bunker was equipped with bunk beds and enough food to support six men for a month or more. A ventilation shaft went through the centre of a thick bush on the hill above.

Roger Weeley recalls the problems he encountered when digging out the bunker.

"First of all I had to 'borrow' a mechanical digger – nothing like the sophisticated things we have today. Much of the main work was done with a pickaxe and shovel. The digger loosened the earth up, then packed it into place on top of the shelter. Not only were we working against time to get the place finished, we had to work as silently as possible to avoid giving the game away and bringing any of the more inquisitive locals to our doorstep."

The Auxiliary Units were to spend the best part of the summer of 1941 preparing bolt-holes and underground bunkers. All told, there would be 3–400 of them scattered around the country.

Yet another East Anglian farmer recruited at the beginning of the scheme was Keith Seabrooke who says he was told to organise a patrol. He set about digging out the bottom of an old tree-girt hole, known locally as The Devil's Pit. Working under cover of darkness, they erected a Nissen hut in the hollow. It collapsed twice under the weight of its covering layer of earth but was eventually completed.

Not officially part of the military, these Auxiliary volunteers were outside the Geneva Convention and would certainly have been shot if captured by the enemy during an invasion. Men were not allowed to carry family photographs or letters to prevent hostage taking by the enemy. Keith Seabrooke recalls that they were regarded as completely expendable. "It was a three-week existence. At the time, I never counted the consequences."

By 1944, Keith Seabrooke's chain of command had grown to embrace 70 patrols stretching from Southend to Cromer. Nearer to home, his beat included the Marconi factory at Colchester, where several of his under-cover operators worked on wireless projects and in secret wireless operations.

Members of the force were involved in a number of hair-raising episodes, mainly involving weapons and explosives. Exercises were carried out

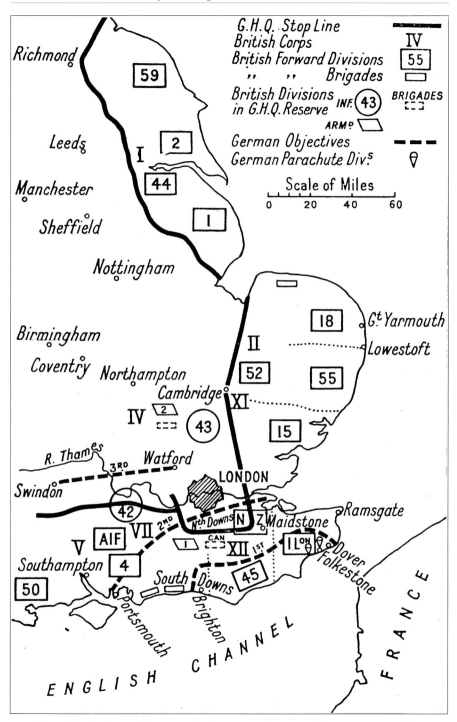

Richmond

59

Leeds

I   2

Manchester

44

Sheffield   I

Nottingham

G.H.Q. Stop Line
British Corps
British Forward Divisions
    ,,   ,,   Brigades
British Divisions
in G.H.Q. Reserve
German Objectives
German Parachute Div.s

IV
55

INF. 43   BRIGADES
ARM.D

18   G.t Yarmouth

Birmingham

II   Lowestoft

Coventry   Northampton

52   55

Cambridge   XI

IV   2
43

15

R. Thames   3RD   Watford

Swindon

LONDON

42

Ramsgate

VII   2ND   N.th Downs   N   Z   Maidstone

V   AIF   I   CAN   XII   1ST   I   L.ON   Dover   Folkestone

Southampton   4   45

50   South Downs   Brighton

Portsmouth

ENGLISH   CHANNEL

FRANCE

Ironside's dispositions and German "Sea Lion" Plan, July 1940.

constantly, mainly at night. In one venture, the Weeley patrol nearly blew themselves to pieces when hanging a selection of home-made mines in trees. Keith Seabrooke recalls the time when a couple of youngsters accidentally stumbled into one of their near-completed bolt-holes, witnessing at first hand the cache of concealed weapons and bombs. Realising that all would be lost if the boys spoke, Seabrooke took them into his confidence and made them swear an oath of silence. Neither culprit has mentioned the adventure since.

In one incident, a new recruit reported to his sergeant armed with a muzzle-loading Brown Bess flintlock dating back to the early 19th century. He complained that although he had managed to procure a lump of flint to jam between the jaws of the cock and had managed to grind down enough red head match for the priming powder, he still couldn't get the gun to spit out the lump of lead he had crammed down the barrel. When asked how much black powder he had poured down the barrel, he replied that he couldn't find any, so had used three inches of cordite instead!

One East Anglian commanding officer turned the pub into a firing range. Arming his men with air rifles, liberated from a closed amusement arcade, they popped away at glass bottles perched on a row of stools at the end of the bar.

Storage of explosives proved a problem, and caches of highly dangerous nitro-glycerine and detonators were sometimes hidden in buried milk churns. Squire Weeley recalls that his men refused to sleep alongside unstable phosphorus bombs or gelignite. These had to be tucked away in easily-accessible waterproof holes outside the bunker.

Sometimes, explosives remained hidden for many years after the war. A few years ago, it was announced in a local paper that a wood in the Tendring district was being cleared for housing. A former member of the 202 Battalion remembered that six churns of nitro had been buried there and alerted the authorities. Royal Engineers, armed with mine detectors

What do I do...

if I have snapshots taken abroad?

I go over them carefully to see if they contain views of scenery or buildings, even as background to personal snaps, because these might be of enormous value in the war-effort.

If I have any such prints I write a brief description of the subjects saying where and roughly when they were taken, and send it to "Photographs", Admiralty, London, S.W.1.

But I do not send the prints themselves until the Admiralty writes for them. I remember that views from *any* foreign land may be useful—town or country scenes, inland or seaside.

Issued by the Ministry of Information

Space presented to the Nation by the Brewers' Society

discovered the unstable, leaking hoard, evacuated the area and despatched the lot in one big bang.

One of the last known large caches of explosives to be discovered dates back to 1964 when a member of the Dengie (Essex) group, Mr Reginald Sennitt, finally decided the time had come to surrender his accumulation of highly lethal stores.

After enrolling in an Auxiliary Unit in 1941, and forming the Dengie group of patrols, responsible for the Bradwell to Southminster marshland, he took on the job of weapons and explosives storemaster. As the marshes were prone to flooding, many of the bolt-holes were unusable, so he decided to keep the explosives in his barn. Worried that they might be spotted by farm hands, he later moved them into the house.

Mr Sennitt and his wife apparently thought nothing of spending nights surrounded by boxes of explosives and primed hand-grenades. By the winter of 1944, much of the major work of the Units had been curtailed. Night after night, men from local groups drove up to the farm to surrender crates of explosives and arms for Sennitt to return to the authorities. No one ever came to collect them, the pile grew and grew, but having signed the Official Secrets Act, Mr Sennitt was reluctant to contact anyone. Taking comfort in the thought that the army couldn't have forgotten, and would one day turn up to collect their stores, he moved the explosives to an unused milking shed, locked up and sat tight.

Time passed. The stores gathered dust. From time to time, Mr Sennitt moved the crates around to allow the stores to 'breathe' as he knew that weeping, sweating explosives had an unsociable habit of blowing up without warning. By 1964 his faith in the army ever turning up was wearing thin and Reg, who had served in the first world war was beginning to feel his age. Off he went to the local police – who were completely nonplussed. Finally, the buck stopped at the Eastern Command Inspectorate in Hounslow.

INVASION – WHY?

Have you any clear idea of the purpose of the attempted invasion of Western Europe?

One thing is certain– the Allied casualties are and will continue to be enormous, although the amount of territory captured will be small.

The only strategic effect that the invasion could have would be to lessen the resistance of the Germans in the East.

If this plan succeeded, Bolshevism would triumph over Europe—and

TRIUMPH OVER BRITAIN AS WELL!

E114 / 3.44

German propaganda leaflet dropped over East Anglia when they, rather than Britain, feared invasion.

On April 7, 1964, a Staff Sergeant of the RASC arrived at the farmhouse and removed the following:

14,378 rounds of ammunition for pistols, rifles and sub-machine guns, including a quantity of incendiary bullets.
1205 lb of gelignite, Nobel 808 and plastic explosive.
3742 ft of delayed action fuse.
930 ft instantaneous safety fuse.
250ft detonating cord.
1447 time pencils.
1207 L-delay switches.
1271 detonators of various types.
791 push, pull and pressure release booby trap switches.
314 paraffin bombs.
340 igniters for the above and for the safety fuses.
131 fog signals.
121 smoke bombs.
212 thunderflashes.
571 primers.
36 1lb slabs of gun cotton.
4 hand-grenades.
10 phosphorus grenades.
33 time switches and booby trap switches attached to made up charges.

The underground army was wound up in 1944, but the British public knew nothing of its existence until the closing stages of the war in Europe, when a message of thanks from Sir Harold Franklyn was published in *The Times* on April 14, 1945.

'*I realise that every member of the organisation, from the first invasion days beginning in 1940, voluntarily undertook a hazardous role which required both skill and courage, knowing that the very nature of their work would allow no public recognition. This organisation, founded on the keenness and patriotism of selected civilians of all grades has been in a position, through its constant and thorough training to furnish accurate information of raids or invasion instantly to military headquarters throughout the country.*'

My prize possessions are two small, battered notebooks kept by Keith Seabrooke during the war. In these, he kept precise details of every man under his command, including records of previous military service, age, and the vehicles they drove.

Now, 47 years after the end of the war, these unsung local heroes can at last be recognised.

EAST ANGLIAN AUXILIARY UNITS 1, GROUP LEADERS

Capt W G Gentle, Brandon, Suffolk.
Capt G Scott-Moncrieff, Hacheston, nr Woodbridge, Suffolk.
Lt J K Field, Woodbridge, Suffolk.
Capt D W Beeton, Woodbridge, Suffolk.
Capt W D G Bartram, Beccles, Suffolk.
Capt H E Mellor, Ipswich, Suffolk.
Capt E G Pawsey, Ipswich, Suffolk.
Lt D G Drake, Bures, Suffolk.
Capt H Rusted, Metfield, Suffolk.
Lt T H Denney, Leiston, Suffolk.
Capt L W O Turner, Kenton, Suffolk.
Capt W K Seabrooke, Great Leighs, Chelmsford, Essex.
Lt H W Gadsby, Kelvedon, Essex.
Capt C G Ford, Hickley, Essex.
Capt R L Sennitt, Dengie, Southminster, Essex.
Capt G H Smith, Colchester, Essex.
Lt J Harper, Colchester, Essex.
Lt H G Dennis, Colchester, Essex.
Capt E J Robinson, King's Lynn, Norfolk.
Lt R R Stanton, Dersingham, King's Lynn, Norfolk.
Capt J L Hardy, DSO, MC, Rougham, King's Lynn, Norfolk.
Lt E G Field, Brandon, King's Lynn, Norfolk.
Lt M Newngs, King's Lynn, Norfolk.
Lt R B St B Wayne, East Dereham, Norfolk.
Lt L N Brock, Walsingham, Norfolk.
Lt G F Rutterford, Brancaster, Norfolk.
Capt H W R Mitchell, Kirby Bedon, Norfolk.
Capt R W Eades, Norwich, Norfolk.
Lt H Wharton, Mautby, Norfolk.
Lt P W Neave, North Walsham, Norfolk.
Capt C N King, MC, Wisbech, Cambs.

The Home Guard and Auxiliary Force alone were not, of course, enough to combat the threat of invasion. Early in the war, General Ironside had decided that a physical barrier against invading troops was needed in susceptible areas like East Anglia.

In the summer of 1940, General Ironside theoretically had at his disposal some 15 infantry divisions, one armoured division, 57 Home Defence battalions and the Local Defence Volunteers. He had very little artillery, since all the new 25 pounders and anti-tank guns had been lost in France. Numbers, equipment, mobility and training were so defective that few units were fit for effective offensive operations. Obviously action was needed.

The General formulated a plan to build a defensive crust along the beaches, backed by blocks and stop lines further inland to prevent armoured penetration. Small fast-moving units would deal with parachutists and airborne troops and there would be a general reserve to the north and west of London for counter attacks towards East Anglia.

In a diary entry dated June 8, he noted:

'.... *as regards airborne expeditions, the Boches have sufficient aircraft to transport 9750 lightly equipped men in one flight. The number of flights per day will vary from one and a half per day for East Anglia to three for Kent. Taking into account air opposition and ground opposition, it is thought that the numbers can be calculated upon the basis of 10,000 for East Anglia and 20,000 for Kent.'*

His inspection of forces from Cromer to King's Lynn on June 20 left little doubt in his mind that *'the work could never end ... it ought to have begun months ago. The great failure is to realise that all the nodal points inland must be fitted with blockhouses to cover big, solid blocks. To restrict all movement in the country, and so prevent enemy columns rushing about the country. I have impressed upon the Government that they ought to be ready with offensive operations if we can see a reasonable chance of upsetting efforts of invasion.'*

Work began on anti-tank obstacles, roadblocks and pillboxes. The public were issued with a Stand Fast leaflet which detailed what to do in case of invasion. The main message was to stay put, hide maps, petrol, food, bicycles or anything else that might help the enemy.

The first line of physical defence stretched along the East Anglian coast, with a second line of road blocks, manned by Home Guard, designed to hold up invading forces.

By the end of June, work was speeded up on the erection of anti-tank obstacles, barbed wire entanglements and pillboxes. One of the most interesting pillboxes was the Pickett-Hamilton Counter Balance Fort for airfields which was designed to house five men. Constructed to be set low in the ground out of the path of operational aircraft, the fort could be raised or lowered by hydraulic jack. Each fort cost £250 and examples were installed on airfields at Stradishall, Wattisham, Bury St Edmunds, Ipswich and Martlesham. Duxford museum has a fully operational model.

Although the majority of pillboxes were built within the shelter of hedgerows or wooded areas, some were camouflaged. Some in coastal regions were disguised as beach huts or bus shelters and, in one instance in the village of Aylsham, as a garden shed.

Several hundred miles of steel scaffolding was erected along the East Anglian coast. Bert Kennell who worked on the project recalls:

Home Guard exercises were frequent in an attempt to prepare for the expected German invasion.

Remains of beach defences in East Anglia.

"I was but one of many who helped to build these steel barriers along the coast. We worked very long hours, up to 12 hours at a time, and earned £7. 10s a week. It was hard, exacting work and often meant standing up to our armpits in freezing water. At low tide we used to dig deep holes into, which loose sided boxes or shutters were slipped to accommodate the first base plate. A special mix of extra-quick-drying cement was then poured in as fast as possible to beat the incoming tide. The next day, the timber was removed to repeat the exercise along the next stretch of beach. We were a mixed bag of workers, the oldest being a man of over 80. Despite his advanced years, he seemed to work much harder than us younger ones."

"My next job was building pillboxes, but soon after they were completed, it was discovered that many of the slit holes had been cast far too large. It was feared that those inside the pillbox would be cut to shreds by a hail of bullets pumped in through the over-sized apertures. My task was to hand-cut slots into the reinforced concrete to take heavy pieces of steel plating. These not only reduced the size of the hole, but also allowed the defenders to slide a protective cover into place if needed."

Explosive charges were laid below the low water line in an attempt to thwart enemy landing barges. On December 15, 1940, during an anti-invasion exercise held at Felixstowe, a self-propelled wooden barge successfully smashed through the barrier without detonating a single charge – much to the dismay of watching service chiefs.

A host of ingenious methods were used in an attempt to stop enemy tanks gaining a foothold on land. Recommendations given to Home Guard commanders suggested that 80 lb steel rails, 5 ft long, should be driven into the ground leaving 2 ft 3 in exposed, and mounds of timber poles stacked 3 ft high and wide securely chained or roped to stakes set 4 ft in the ground. On winding country roads, holes were dug into the tarmac to take specially cast concrete and steel traps capable of holding up-ended lengths of railway track when the road needed to be closed against enemy traffic. Deep anti-tank ditches were evacuated on open marshland. The most common of these was V-shaped, 5 ft deep, 12 ft wide and believed to be effective against 25 ton tanks. The earth dug from the hole was used to raise one side, making an awesome drop of 11 ft into a water filled ditch.

Concrete obstacles were built right along the coast. In East Anglia, the most common were pyramids and cubes. Many can still be seen in rural areas.

General Ironside's GHQ line of pillboxes and other obstacles stretched from Great Chesterford, south east through Great Dunmow, Chelmsford, Battlebridge and Benfleet to run alongside the Thames at Canvey Island. Another stop line began at the ancient shipyard of Wivenhoe, meandered through Colchester, then through to Sudbury and Bury St Edmunds.

In 1940, coastal defences were very much the same as during the First World War. The most vulnerable area was the stretch of water between

Above: *Home Guard insignia and certificate*
Right: *A member of the East Anglian TA seen on exercise during the early part of the war.*
Below: *Kirby Cross ARP.*

St Osyth and Walton-on-the-Naze. Five emergency batteries were built to protect river mouths and poorly defended coastal regions. A 6 in battery was installed at Frinton, and there were two ex-naval 6 in guns at nearby Holland-on-Sea. Two 4.7 in batteries were built at either end of Mersea Island to protect the Colne and the Blackwater.

At the naval docks in Harwich, two 12 pounders were mounted in brick and concrete gunhouses disguised as fishermen's cottages at Angle Gate. AA guns encircled the town, and two 6 in Mk VIII's were erected in open emplacements at Beacon Hill. A line of machine-gun posts, anti-tank obstacles and pillboxes stretched from Dovercourt to the Stour near Parkeston Quay, supported with an array of 75 mm guns, 6 and 2 pounder anti-tank guns and 25 pounders.

Just across the Orwell at Felixstowe, two large 9.2 in guns had already been installed at Brackenbury Battery when hostilities opened. An emergency battery was sited to the north of Landguard Fort, opposite the Manor House Hotel. Land defences were hurriedly constructed in 1940, with anti-tank weapons covering the marshes and also the town. Landguard Fort itself  had two 12 pounders and fixed beam searchlights.

In Suffolk, emergency beach batteries were built at Sizewell, Dunwich, Covehithe and Pakefield. Later, additional batteries appeared at Bawdsey, Hopton and Kessingland. All positions boasted secondary armament for close defence work, usually 7 mm guns, rocket projectors and light AA guns. A series of pillboxes, mines, steel barriers and other obstacles ran along the beach between the batteries. More pillboxes were erected further inland. Along the River Waveney, there was a pillbox at every crossing, with a second line of defence formed by the Hundred River from Kessingland to Beccles. The all-important defence line stretched right through Suffolk from Colchester, Bures, Sudbury, Lavenham and Bury St Edmunds to Mildenhall.

In Norfolk, AA practice camps were built at Weybourne and Stiffkey – much to the dismay of local inhabitants who raised such a fuss that General Ironside was forced to appear in person to try and smooth things over. In 1940, emergency gun and searchlight batteries were installed at Hunstanton, High Cape, Holkham Bay, Cley, Eye, Sheringham, Cromer, Happisburgh and

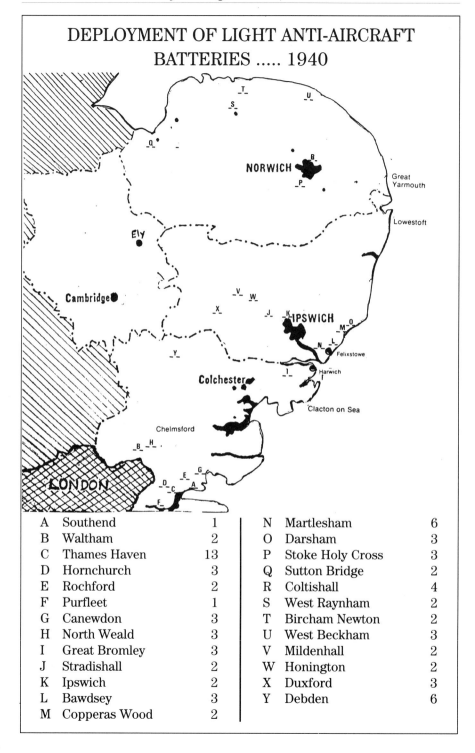

DEPLOYMENT OF LIGHT ANTI-AIRCRAFT BATTERIES 1940

A	Southend	1	N	Martlesham	6
B	Waltham	2	O	Darsham	3
C	Thames Haven	13	P	Stoke Holy Cross	3
D	Hornchurch	3	Q	Sutton Bridge	2
E	Rochford	2	R	Coltishall	4
F	Purfleet	1	S	West Raynham	2
G	Canewdon	3	T	Bircham Newton	2
H	North Weald	3	U	West Beckham	3
I	Great Bromley	3	V	Mildenhall	2
J	Stradishall	2	W	Honington	2
K	Ipswich	2	X	Duxford	3
L	Bawdsey	3	Y	Debden	6
M	Copperas Wood	2			

Winterton. A shortage of mobile artillery pieces meant that many ancient relics were pressed into service. In Norfolk, several guns dated back to the turn of the century. One Winterton battery bore 1909 proof marks. Pillboxes protected the Ant, Bure, Acle, Yare and Waveney.

Norwich was the command post and nerve centre of the East Anglian defence operation. During the summer months of the Battle of Britain, a defensive perimeter of pillboxes, roadblocks, anti-tank traps and other barriers was thrown around the city. AA guns were added in 1940.

At Great Yarmouth, two 12 pounders were established at the end of the south pier as a protection against E-boat attacks, with a 40 mm Bofors on the north pier. Another important battery (the 'Links' battery) stood on the cliffs at Gorleston, about a mile south of the harbour entrance.

Not all the batteries had been well planned. At King's Lynn, pillboxes, road blocks and tank traps were protected by 6 in guns installed on the marshes by the Ouse. Unfortunately, the planners had not allowed for the wide sweep of the tide and had set the guns well out of range of any likely target venturing up river.

By July 1940, the GHQ Stop Line in East Anglia was well in hand, ready for the invasion which, incredible as it seems now, was expected any day.

CHAPTER FOUR

Civilians at War

*T*his was the first war to really involve civilians. True, East Anglians and Londoners had experienced visits from Gotha and Zeppelin bombers in the First World War, but this time everyone from the family pet upwards was affected by rationing, regulations, shortages of clothing, hardware and other essentials, and by the restrictions of national security.

By 1940, U-boat raids on shipping meant that almost everything was rationed – even cigarettes. A utility cigarette, colourfully known as a 'Pasha', was introduced. One Lowestoft policeman was convinced that it was made from camel dung. A Frinton smoker was driven to the extreme measure of experimenting with chrysanthemum leaves which he dried, then rolled up into foul smelling cigarettes. During the war, he experimented with all sorts of leaves and plants. He swore by blackberry leaves but confessed that chopped straw mixed with lavender and geranium leaves nearly killed him!

Bored soldiers cashed in on the match shortage by turning spent .303 rifle cartridges into lighters. Table lighters were made from used cannon, mortar and Bofors shell cases, many bearing ornate scrimshaw work setting out regimental histories, battle engagements and town names.

Drink was also in short supply and many public houses were forced to introduce rationing. The price of beer rose steadily throughout the war. By 1944, it was 1s 3d (7p) a pint. Spirits were over 25s (£1.25) a bottle legally; four times that on the black market. Many tried to brew their own hooch. On one East Anglian airbase coloured American servicemen kept the nearby town supplied by manufacturing their own Scotch which relied on high octane aircraft fuel for its kick. The team was highly organised and even had colourful labels for the bottles. The leader, it was later discovered, had been a famed moonshine runner back home in the USA.

In the main, the public accepted shortages – but rationed items or other goods in short supply could be obtained at a price. In an East Anglian newspaper for 1941, the Wanted columns were full and the For Sale column almost empty. One Little Clacton farm worker spent his leisure hours dragging abandoned bicycles from the hedges, cleaning and repairing them and selling them for £6 each – a week's wages in those days.

The war was to breed a character new to British life ..... the spiv. Typically dressed in a loud suit, co-respondent shoes, garish tie and snap-brimmed hat, these characters always seemed to have a pencil moustache and lavishly Brylcreemed hair. Spivs acted as go-betweens in black market transactions and seemed to know where, and how, to lay their hands on just about anything. Almost every large town had its spivs. In East Anglia, they could be seen in the pubs, clinching shady deals with certain gentlemen farmers, market gardeners or American servicemen.

Black market activities weren't restricted to civvy street. In 1942, at a Colchester court martial, four officers of the RASC were dismissed from the service for certain irregularities. These included receiving coal and paraffin, improperly drawing servant's allowances, stealing food and permitting repairs to be done to private cars by soldiers and civilians in an RASC workshop. This was just the tip of the iceberg.

Rolls of barbed wire, field kitchens, timber, motor tyres and even typewriters disappeared from military stores to re-appear on the open market. In some cases, whole crates of tinned food were stolen and buried in slit trenches to be retrieved at a later date and sold to hotels, restaurants or anyone with ready cash and a still tongue.

One colourful character who worked on the laying of heavy-duty searchlight cable along the clifftops of Harwich, Frinton and Walton kept a detailed plan of the actual location of each stretch of cable and returned soon after the war to dig them up. He cut the valuable copper wire into strips, ready to be sold when prices rose.

The self-same entrepreneur was party to a wartime black market fiddle involving the theft of WD engines while he was serving as a civilian engineer at an army motor pool.

"You must understand that owning or driving a car was almost unheard of unless you were on war work or some other important job" he explained. "Even then, the chances of getting the necessary extra petrol coupons to allow you to use the vehicle for anything other than work were slim. Engine spares were certainly unheard of, and anyone who had access to anything in that line could command their own price. That's where we came in. We were surrounded by tyres, batteries, springs, wheels, brand new engines, everything you could ask for. There were three of us in on the racket, including a motor pool officer who would sign anything for a quid or two."

"The way it operated was like this. Imagine an army lorry, a staff car or even a motor bike being brought in with engine problems. The rule was strip it down, mend it if possible or, if not, put in for a new engine or parts. It was left to us to decide what was best and quickest. Of course, I'm talking about well into the war when a lot of stuff was being shipped over from the States

Norwich children threw themselves into the drive for scrap metal.

The Cadbury's cocoa van brought much-needed comfort to bombed-out civilians and the rescue workers.

and Canada, and the stores were full to overflowing. If the engine we just happened to be working on was something we could place out on the street, we did no more than issue a ticket saying that it was beyond repair and we needed a replacement. Our officer buddy would then issue the proper paper work, which allowed us to pick up a new engine from the stores. The way it worked was really quite simple. In the forces, everything works on a replacement value. If you wore out a uniform or a pair of boots, you could have a replacement if you had the right piece of paper, plus the worn out item. We drew the new engine, fitted it to the vehicle, then stacked the old one out in the yard. But before it was collected, we'd swopped it for an engine from one of the hundreds of old cars left rusting in fields and barns. Sometimes, I would just stockpile spares and by the end of the war we had enough stuff to start a workshop."

A lot of tales have circulated about black market enterprises. One of the funniest concerns an East Anglian pigswill man. He had a working understanding with a cook at one of the camps he visited daily to collect swill. For an undisclosed sum, the cook would leave a few off-ration items hidden in the waste. A keen police inspector heard of this and decided to have a surprise vehicle check at the camp gates. Standing majestically in front of the evil smelling load, the inspector ordered the lot to be tipped out. Imagine his fury when all he found was potato peelings and fish heads. Luckily for the swill man, the cook was off sick with food poisoning!

Petrol was another popular black market commodity. For those not prepared to deal with the spivs, the idea of gas propulsion seemed the ideal solution to the fuel shortage. The Fuel Research Station and British Coal Utilisation Research Association advocated the use of gas, anthracite or coke

and planned to set up a series of supply points at strategic positions around large towns.

The gas powered car carried its fuel in a large bag on the roof. Gas cars had been used during the First World War, but as the bag flopped over the windscreen as it deflated, their use was not popular. The problem was solved this time round by encasing the bag in a bellows structure which allowed the material to fold back in place. The cost of filling this 9 ft by 6 ft by 4 ft encumbrance with the equivalent of a gallon of petrol was £30.

The gas powered car was banned in 1942 because of fuel shortages. Instead, commercial vehicles were equipped with a producer-gas generator towed behind on a trailer. The burner looked like a large dustbin on wheels and devoured a ton of anthracite a week. It needed frequent overhauls and maintenance. The burner was first introduced in East Anglia by a Mr M Morrison who tried it out at Maldon on the Eastern National Bus Company. Passengers in Colchester will no doubt remember how red hot coke used to bounce out and set the pitch-soaked wooden road blocks on fire at the East Gates level crossing – a hazard at night, especially when a raid was on.

Radio shows such as *ITMA*, and films like *Goodbye Mr Chips* helped to keep the war-weary public entertained. Live entertainment outside London was restricted to amateur groups and volunteer organisations. The City of Norwich owes much to the police concert party which raised funds for blitz victims and dependants of men from stricken ships.

The majority of professional entertainers had volunteered for service with

ENSA – 'every night something awful' according to jokers. During the early days, Rex Newman, producer of pre-war seaside hit, Fol-de-Rols took the first batch of ENSA concert parties to troops stationed in remote corners of the country. With costumes, instruments and odd bits of hastily built scenery in the back of lorries, they spent Christmas slipping and sliding around East Anglia's icy roads.

One of East Anglia's ENSA stars was Norman Lynn, comedian and ukulele player of Walton. He served all over Britain, including the Orkneys and Shetlands and accompanied the advancing Allies into Europe.

KEEPS WAR WORKERS "FIGHTING FIT"

Fitness means EVERYTHING to them

That is why Weetabix is so popular in the canteens. It gives them stamina—staying power! Besides, Weetabix is so delicious, whether eaten dry or with a "spread." And so easily digested, too.

Weetabix is the *whole* of the wheat. All the health-giving vitamins and mineral salts so richly found in wheat are effectively preserved in Weetabix. Make a habit of eating some Weetabix every day—at home or at the canteen—and you'll be delighted to find how much fitter you are for the strenuous work you have to do.

Weetabix
More than a breakfast food

Weetabix Ltd., Burton Latimer, Northants.

Small Size 7½d.
2 POINTS
Double Size 1/1d.
4 POINTS
W.X.6

Equally comforting to troops and war workers was the NAAFI. The Norwich NAAFI club, built on the bombed site of Buntings in Rampant Horse Street was considered to be one of the best in East Anglia as it had a dance floor, billiard and table-tennis rooms, a sewing room and a luxurious bar.

Even children could 'do their bit'. Fired by patriotism, gangs of youngsters were organised into salvage groups known as Cogs. The Cogs scavenged for waste paper and scrap metal, textiles, bottles, skins, old bones – in fact anything which could be re-cycled. Over 600 tons of scrap valued at over £600 was collected in Norwich in 24 weeks. The children's theme song was "*there'll always be a dustbin* ...."

Salvage mania reached fever pitch when Beaverbrook announced that even pots and pans, or indeed any items made wholly or partly of aluminium could become Spitfires and Hurricanes. The trouble was that much of the scrap collected was mixed metal. As manpower was short, the scrap was carted away to central dumps and abandoned. The British Aluminium Company in the Midlands still had wartime mixed scrap as late as the 1960's.

Aluminium wasn't the only metal wanted by Whitehall. When the call went out for scrap iron and steel, many fine gates and railings were sacrificed from historical properties around East Anglia and were never replaced.

The Spitfire Fund was yet another Beaverbrook scheme. The idea was that towns and villages should raise funds to buy a plane. The name of the town would be painted on the side of the aircraft. By 1943, Save Weeks were all the rage with War Weapons, Salute the Soldier, Wings for Victory and Thanksgiving Week. One idea which turned sour on the organisers was the plan to ask a private soldier to take the salute at Harwich in Salute the Soldier week. The War Office frowned on such a 'bolshie' idea, compromising by allowing an NCO to sit beside the high ranking officers on the saluting base.

Eligible civilians not in uniform in the early days didn't suffer the white feather treatment of the First World War. However, once Dunkirk was in the news, conscientious objectors became the focus of media attention. Angry letters appeared in local papers, accusing 'conchies' of being 'gutless' and belonging to the 'funk brigade'. County councillors and other Anglian worthies tried to have 'conchies' working for the council dismissed. Some Union officials forgot principles of fair play and workers' rights and threatened strike action unless 'conchies' were removed from the workforce.

Walton entertainer Norman Lynn travelled around Britain and Europe with ENSA.

For some reason, Norwich had the highest number of conscientious objectors in the country, and city newspapers carried large numbers of for and against letters and articles.

With bombing threatened, civilians needed some form of air raid shelter. Public shelters were built, of course, and trenches were dug on golf courses, parks and open land. More appealing to families was the small Anderson shelter, available free to anyone earning under £250 a year, £10 to the better off. The Anderson was made of curved sections of corrugated steel standing on thick girders and sunk about 3 ft into the ground. The top of the Anderson was covered with a thick layer of earth or with sandbags. The sunken entrance was protected by a steel shield and earthen blast wall. Six people could shelter in the Anderson. Equipped with bunk beds, it could even be described as comfortable – and could withstand almost anything bar a direct hit. Rail travellers using the Ipswich to Norwich line can still see several Andersons tucked at the bottom of allotment gardens, nestling close to the railway fence.

When the V-1 and V-2 raids started later in the war, many opted for the indoor Morrison shelter. This was a large steel cage, with solid top and sides of heavy gauge wire mesh. During the day, it could be covered with a tablecloth. The Morrison could hold three adults and one child, but in practice more, including the family pet, were usually crammed in.

CHAPTER FIVE

Down on the Farm

With shipping badly hit by U-boats, it was vital that every inch of land should be farmed as effectively as possible to keep the national larder filled. In 1940, the Minister of Agriculture appealed for a further two million acres to be put under the plough, and by the end of 1944, nearly seven million extra acres had been turned to agriculture. Even the Ford Motor Company at Dagenham did its bit for agriculture, giving the 170 acres known as Lake Farm for allotments, rented out to employees at 7s 6d a year. At the Henry Ford Institute of Agricultural Engineering near Colchester, young lads and the Women's Land Army (WLA) received agricultural training.

Life was far from easy for East Anglian farmers. In many cases, derelict land was beyond reclamation. In Norfolk, 50,000 acres of land, set aside in the 30s slump had turned to scrub. Much of the area had been turned over to raising game birds for shooting. In Suffolk, well over 40,000 acres was given over to game preservation, a legacy of Edward VII and his sporting land baron friends. Farmhouses lay derelict and abandoned, roofs patched with tar paper and sacking. The war agricultural committees worked wonders in clearing the land and repairing property.

Drainage was a great problem. Small farmers were unable to cope with the task of reclaiming waterlogged land, and the army was called in to help.

Land Army girls were called in to help with this heavy work – East Anglia was one of the first areas to see these new agricultural workers. Made up of girls from all walks of life, the WLA were a hard-working lot. On joining, every girl was supplied with two green jerseys, two pairs of breeches, two overall coats, two pairs of dungarees, six pairs of stockings, three shirts, one pair of ankle boots, one pair of shoes, one pair of gumboots or shoes with leggings, one hat, one overcoat with shoulder titles, one mackintosh or oilskin, two towels, one oilskin sou'wester, a green armlet and a metal badge, ready for work on the land.

The girls worked on hedging, haymaking, harvesting, milking and looking after stock. They were also expected to cope with gassed or shell-shocked farm animals. In the early part of the war, gas attack was expected daily. The girls had to keep a supply of dampened sacks and cloths to lay over chicken coops, kennels and cowshed windows. If the fields had been sprayed with lewisite or mustard gas, the farmer and WLA were to lead the blistered cattle in from the fields and treat them with a solution of bicarbonate of soda. Sores were to be annointed with a bleach ointment. Thankfully, gas attacks did not materialise, but the WLA was ready for the worst.

Many of the girls learned to plough, and during the Dig for Victory campaign, could be seen working at night using the light from a lantern hidden in a ditch or tied to the plough.

Not all farmers took kindly to being told what to plough. Land girls were often employed in labour gangs working under the control of the County War Agricultural Executive Committee which put Ministry of Agriculture policy into action – much to the disgust of some farmers.

Helen Barker, who was a Land girl in Norfolk, recalls working on dragging fossilised tree stumps out of overgrown swampland.

"Despite the fact that we all wore heavy gumboots and mackintoshes, we were all soaking wet within the first half hour of starting work. It was terribly hard work. I can still remember the stench of rotting wood and stagnant water. It was like wading through thick black and brown soup. During the long months of double summer time, we were plagued by thousands of gnats and midges, all intent on stinging and biting us to death. After work, we spent our time dabbing the bites with vinegar or, if we could find any, calamine lotion. We must have looked a sight and I'm sure nobody but a blind man could have fancied any of us."

Land girls were also expected to act as rodent catchers – and were very effective as an Essex farmer remembers.

"A pretty, shapely young thing who'd flutter her eyelashes at anything in trousers took an absolute delight in despatching rats. The look on her face as she finished them off convinced me not to get the wrong side of her."

Nothing stopped the Land girls. It was a common sight in Norfolk and Suffolk to see a tin-hatted girl blithely driving a tractor while a dogfight raged overhead. Girls often helped to pull airmen from crashed aircraft, and dealt with rick and barn fires caused by incendiary bombs.

Farming under pressure to produce more and more food was not the easiest of lives – but there were compensations. Producing eggs, butter, cheese, milk and meat meant that the family didn't go without, and farmer's wives were great hands at making home-made wine and beer from all manner of strange fruits and roots.

Not everyone kept news of home-produced delicacies to themselves, as a Suffolk character known as Old Jack discovered to his cost.

Having enjoyed a few pints of local ale, Old Jack enjoyed himself boasting about a special pig, slaughtered for his son's wedding and tucked away from

The Pie Scheme, organised by the ladies of the WVS, provided food for agricultural workers.

the prying eyes of the Ministry of Agriculture inspector. Unfortunately, Jack didn't notice two strangers in the corner of the bar, and it wasn't until he arrived home, the worse for drink, that he realised that they had followed him. One of the pair pulled an official looking card from his pocket and told Jack that he was a Ministry inspector, come to claim the pig. He warned Jack that he would be issued with a summons in a few days. So far, Jack is still waiting ....

Agricultural workers needed good, filling food to keep them working hard. In 1941, East Anglia saw the launch of the Pie Scheme which was introduced in Cambridge. The WVS organised mass distribution of pies to agricultural workers gathering in the harvest. Delivering food direct to the field meant that time was saved, and workers were fed with minimum disruption and loss of working hours.

CHAPTER SIX

Industry at War

*I*ndustry was swiftly turned over to war production - and many East Anglian firms 'did their bit' in the desperate race to make aircraft and armaments.

Ford at Dagenham produced all sorts of wheeled vehicles for the Forces. Just 35 miles away in Colchester, wireless experts Marconi tackled the daunting task of perfecting the newly introduced radar and communications systems. At Colchester, Davey, Paxman & Co Ltd developed munitions and machinery – as did Ransomes, Sims & Jeffries in Ipswich. Boulton and Paul in Norwich built hundreds of air-raid shelters, radio masts, tank transporters and made thousands of yards of Sommerfield wire-woven netting which was used to lay landing strips on grass, sand and emergency airfields.

War production didn't start immediately. Although Ford was ready to move into full emergency gear, the normal 40 hours a week continued for quite some time after the outbreak of war.

Many industries developed complex plans for the destruction of machinery should the invasion come. At Ford, every member of the ARP staff had specific instructions on what to do and when to do it. Operational orders were issued to the heads of some departments, giving details on how benzole stocks were to be disrupted, petrol immobilised, the blast furnace shut down and spares and drawings removed. The power house was to be made useless by hiding important parts. Diesel engines, completed vehicles and water pumps were to be sabotaged. This plan of careful and methodical destruction could only be put into operation by use of a series of secret coded messages.

Once bombing started in earnest, Ford introduced a special 'alarm within the alert' system. Prior to the introduction of this scheme in January 1941, there had been an enormous loss of working hours as staff took cover during raids. Under the alarm within the alert system, spotters were linked by phone to AA batteries and information from the gunners was plotted by ARP staff, so that the sirens were only sounded when aircraft were obviously heading for Dagenham and the Ford complex.

Ford was, of course, a prime target for enemy pilots – and easy to find as the factory was on the banks of the Thames. On September 21, 1940, 284 incendiary bombs fell on the factory. Later in the war, 79 flying bombs crashed and exploded in the vicinity. During the closing stages of the war, factory spotters tagged 579 V2's.

Like many other factories, Ford's was camouflaged, but it was hard to hide tall chimneys and a blast furnace. Various experts tried their best by painting a marshland scene on the rooftops of the larger buildings. Metal sheeting covered the coke ovens, and the mountain of slag stacked close to the factory perimeter was encircled by a metal cage designed to prevent the glare being reflected in the night sky.

Workers were well cared for, with canteens throughout the factory. Ford did its bit for the civilian population too. Ford Emergency Food Vans, fitted with a pie oven and a tea urn were a godsend to many in the blitz.

Ford workers took great pride in the vehicles they produced – especially Dagenham Daisy. This was a 15 cwt truck, produced in 1943 and driven by a Dagenham man, Trooper J Knowles. Up to D-Day, the truck had travelled 19,000 miles around the country roads of East Anglia. On D-Day plus two, she joined the Seventh Armoured Division on the beach head. Loaded with rations and supplies for tank crews, she arrived at a little wood near Tilly with her canvas cover ripped to shreds by shrapnel. A month later, her cab cover was riddled and a front tyre shredded when she was strafed. A few days later when taking supplies to Caen, Daisy came under intensive mortar fire, but survived a bumpy getaway down a bomb-cratered cart track.

That night, enemy bombers dropped anti-personnel bombs close by. Splinters peppered Daisy's bonnet, destroying the air filter and slicing the fan belt in two, but she was back on the road within 24 hours.

Despite heavy bombing, Ford produced 347,371 vehicles during the war, and was instrumental in the production of an engine waterproofer called Trinadite. In the week January 7–15, 1944, 200 troop carriers rolled off the production line.

Wireless firms started war work right at the beginning. Marconi installed SWB8 high frequency transmitters and assorted communications equipment in commandeered motor coaches, ready to be despatched to France with the BEF. These mobile radio stations were the only means of communication between the troops and the War Office during the retreat to Dunkirk. Just one SWB8 survived. It was rebuilt by Marconi and used again.

Marconi installed electrical equipment in Whitley, Blenheim, Wellington and Hampden bombers. During the early years of the war, Marconi engineers were formed into five special units to re-equip over 2000 combat aircraft.

Marconi Marine had about 2000 radio officers on the staff in 1939. By autumn 1940, this number had increased to 6000. These men maintained

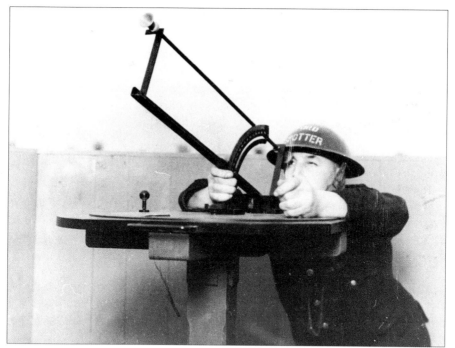

Spotter at the Ford Dagenham works.

Ford workers carrying out repairs after bombing.

communications and assisted navigation in Marconi-equipped merchant ships – a dangerous job thanks to U-boat attacks.

Paxmans of Colchester supplied engines for landing craft, and were responsible for building the engines for a motorised trench digger known as Nellie. Measuring 77 ft long, 6 ft 6 in wide and 5 ft high, Nellie was the brainchild of Winston Churchill and was intended to be one of 250 diggers designed to provide cover for troops crossing the no-man's land up to the Siegfried Line. The idea was to move the diggers under the cover of a concentrated gun barrage which would hide the noise of their progress as troops moved nearer enemy lines.

Norwich suffered terribly during the blitz, but Boulton and Paul continued production, undaunted by heavy bombing. In July 1940, the Riverside Works was bombed, killing ten people and injuring 68. Workshops were destroyed in subsequent raids. Despite this, Boulton continued to produce various items made from steel and wooden parts for the Horsa glider used to transport airborne troops.

Marshall of Cambridge had close links with flying. Founded in 1909, by David Gregory Marshall, the company came into its own, when from a garage in Jesus Lane, it maintained and repaired military vehicles. In 1929, Arthur Marshall started the first Cambridge aerodrome. By 1937, the business had been transferred to the new Cambridge Airport, where the Marshall Flying Training School was responsible for many new pilots. During the war years, over 20,000 pilots, instructors and observers trained at Marshall schools. Over 5000 aircraft were repaired or converted by Marshalls during the war.

Just how active Marshalls were at this time can be seen in these extracts from its official history:

Bombs on Cambridge
In the early years of the war, it was thought that, as a result of its easterly location, the Company would be bombed out and not survive long. In the event, the aerodrome was raided twice only, with limited damage to Tiger Moths, Oxfords and a Lysander. It was rumoured locally that the pilot of the first raider, a Dornier 215, was an ex-Cambridge undergraduate who knew his way around.

Air raid patrols
Peter May, the Company's Chief Flying Instructor of 22 EFTS was always full of fun and bright ideas. During the Battle of Britain, when the Company was repairing Gladiator aircraft, he had managed to scrounge some ammunition and thought it would be a good idea if two Gladiators were available for flight test during air raid warnings, so that he and Arthur Marshall could take to the air to protect the aerodrome and encourage the workers to continue working during raids. The plan went into action on

three occasions, but the problem was to know when the all-clear had been sounded. During air raid warnings, buses remained stationary. As soon as the buses started moving, the raid was over and the planes could land.

Armed Tiger Moths

The Company was instructed to fit bomb racks to Tiger Moths to carry eight 20 lb anti-personnel bombs under each wing for use against invading forces. The plan was to fly just above ground level until the enemy was identified, then to climb to 800 ft, dive to 500 ft, release the bombs and fly home.

Practice was attempted by throwing bricks over the side, but the bricks fell faster than the diving plane, risking damage to the propeller. An instruction was given to eject the bricks very forcibly away from the rear of the aircraft. This was known as the Banquet Light Scheme.

Training by night

In January 1942, following discussions with the C-in-C Training Command, six pupils who had never flown before were allocated to Cambridge for night only training. Three were trained on instruments, following much Link Trainer instruction, and the other three were trained by a more conventional mix of instrument and visual flying. All the pupils got off solo after an average of about 15 hours dual. Those who had been trained on instruments only were found to be put off by bright moonlight. After completing about 30 hours of flying only at night, the pupils were taught to fly by day, following which they were passed for special night flying instruction to the SFTS at Cranwell. This experiment blew away the last remnants of night flying at Elementary Flying Schools.

Defence of Cambridge Airport

The Company was unsuccessful in its attempts to obtain a Swedish Bofors 40 mm anti-aircraft gun. The airfield's only protection was from two machine-guns, one fixed, one mobile. Two Austin 12 cars were armoured, using boiler plate, and used for defence.

The aerodrome had its own Home Guard unit, ARP organisation and gas decontamination centre. During the Battle of Britain, all instructors and students were rostered to carry out security patrols from 0300 to one hour after sunrise. They then had breakfast and went straight on to flying duties. In 1940, cadets of the Air Defence Cadet Corps were called in to help

Railways were vital in transporting goods from the factories to the forces, and in keeping communications open across the region. Attack from the air was nothing new to East Anglian railwaymen. During the First World War, as they crossed the coast, Zeppelin pilots homed in on the sparks and glow from engine fireboxes. Things didn't improve during the second world war as lines, goods yards, stations and trains were machine-gunned, strafed and bombed by the enemy.

Yarmouth South Town station had a narrow escape on May 7, 1942, when a 500 kg bomb fell on the main line but failed to explode. Fortunately, there was a naval bomb disposal officer en-route to his home on a nearby train, and he defused the bomb.

At Barnham on the Bury St Edmunds to Thetford line, a special siding was built for ICI. It is estimated that over 720,000 tons of munitions were handled there during the war years.

The line from Cambridge to Chappel and Wakes Colne was constantly busy transporting tons of brick rubble from bombed buildings as foundations for the new airfield at Wormingford. A high octane petrol depot was built to ferry supplies to the airfield twice daily. Extra long sidings were built at Earsham for RAF stores. Around 200,000 tons of essential supplies passed through this siding.

At Aldeburgh, the line was patrolled by trains armoured with six pounder guns salvaged from First World War tanks. The Southwold railway further along the coast was cut when the swing bridge across the River Blyth was dismantled during the invasion scare.

The railway had its fair share of heroes, and several men of the LNER were awarded medals. The oldest, John Steel won the George Medal for his part in the rescue of rolling stock from his station.

George Brown, then Assistant Traffic Agent, aged 50 and with 35 years of railway service behind him, said shortly afterwards:

"It was a very hot spot with flames from the pit props blowing over in the strong wind. Ten ammo wagons were at the bottom of the yard, and we had to get them away from the fire before they blew up."

A woman munitions worker at Elliott & Garrood, Beccles.

Baking for the troops at Wattisham.

"Inspectors Hume and Colthorpe, engine driver John Steel, goods-guard Ward and shunter Angus were there. Hume said John Steel was willing to use his engine and could run it single handed."

"Our first job was to get six loco engines into shelter. Bombs were sending up timber and debris on all sides. As the bombs dropped, we dipped under the wagons. I saw one man standing by his crane, blown into the water then picked out and saved. Road by road we cleared the yard. Colthorpe and I worked on the couplings with Angus. Hume and Steel were directing and driving and said they couldn't see us at times because of the flames. Ward, one of our best men, worked in every capacity. He had no helmet. His cap had a dozen holes burned in it. Colthorpe should have gone off at midnight, but he worked on until he had completed 16 hours. We all mucked in together, shunting, coupling and putting out fires. The signalman was splendid. His place was blown in, but he stuck to it and went right through it unhurt. The flames were licking over the ammo wagons while we were taking them away."

Steel was given the George Medal for his part in this action. George, Brown, Colthorpe and Angus all received the BEM.

CHAPTER SEVEN

The War at Sea

*O*fficially, Operation Dynamo, the evacuation of the BEF from beleaguered Dunkirk began on Sunday, May 26, 1940 and ended on June 3 at 3.40 am when the destroyer *Shikari* left the East Mole crammed with the last of the Allied forces.

In an official communique soon after the rescue operation, the Admiralty stated:

'The most extensive and difficult combined operation in naval history has been carried out during the past week. British, French and Belgian troops have been brought safely to this country from Belgium and Northern France in numbers which, when the full story can be told, will surprise the world. The withdrawal has been carried out in the face of intense and almost continuous air attack, artillery and machine gun fire. The success of this operation was only made possible by the close co-operation of the Allies and of the Services, and by the never-flagging determination of all concerned. It was undertaken on the British side by several flotillas of destroyers and a large number of small craft of every description. This force was rapidly increased and a total of 222 British naval vessels and 665 other British craft took part. Through the operation of the Small Craft Registration Order, the Admiralty already had full details of all available small vessels. The order for the assembly of the vessels met with instantaneous response. Fishermen, yachtsmen, yacht builders, yacht clubs, river boatmen and boat hire firms manned their craft with volunteer crews and rushed them to the assembly point, although they did not then know for what purpose they were required. They operated successfully by day and by night under the most difficult and dangerous conditions. The Admiralty cannot speak too highly of the services of all concerned. They were essential to the success of the operation and the means of saving thousands of lives.'

Altogether, 1432 vessels, including 19 RNLI lifeboats, took part in the evacuation. Many of the smaller, privately owned craft were never officially requisitioned. Some went of their own accord. Several vanished during the Channel crossing, unrecorded and unknown.

One man stranded at Dunkirk didn't wait for the boats to arrive, but took matters into his own hands. Regular soldier Roy Pagani, serving with the BEF, didn't fancy waiting around on the beaches, so he 'borrowed' a small sailing dinghy and set sail, eventually landing at Bawdsey.

Many East Anglian craft went to Dunkirk with the rescue armada:

Resolute, gaff cutter (Bawley), cockle sailing ship from Leigh-on-Sea. The Bawleys were flat-bottomed, broad-beamed gaff sail cutters around 36 ft long, designed primarily to be beached on sandbanks at high tide, allowing fishermen to clamber over the side to gather shrimps and cockles.

Renown, also from Leigh-on-Sea struck a mine with the loss of skipper Harry Noakes, and crew Frank and Leslie Osborne and Harold G Porter. A memorial can be found at St Clement's Church, Leigh.

Reliance, cockle boat skippered by A Legget.

Defender, built in 1920 this cockle boat went to Dunkirk under command of Sub Lt Soloman, RNVR with *Endeavour, Renown, Letitia, Reliance* and *Resolute*.

Endeavour played an important part in embarking soldiers from the beach. Her rudder was damaged and she was towed back to England by the drifter *Ben & Lucy*.

Letitia, an auxiliary motor sailer, 30 ft long was damaged off Dunkirk but towed to safety by *Ben & Lucy*.

Tollesbury, a barge built in 1901, 84 ft long and made from pitch pine on an oak frame was part of the famous R & W Paul fleet. *Tollesbury* was pressed into war service to assist with the Dunkirk evacuation. Originally, it had been intended to use barges as embarkation platforms by beaching them on the sands to allow stranded soldiers access to smaller craft. Once 250 soldiers were aboard, skipper Lemon Webb took a gamble, re-floated the barge and after running a hail of machine-gun fire and bombs, survived a close encounter with a mine to reach Ramsgate.

Ethel Maud, sailing barge from Maldon. Thought to be a supply vessel.

Ena, spritsail barge built at Harwich in 1906, taken to Dunkirk as a supply boat skippered by A Page.

Greta, barge out of Brightlingsea built by Stones in 1892. Served during the war as an ammunition carrier and took part in the evacuation.

Oulton Belle, motor vessel built at Great Yarmouth in 1940.

Norwich Belle, 90 ton excursion steamer, part of the Yarmouth and Gorleston Steamboat Co fleet. Served later in the war as a fireboat at Lowestoft.

Lucy Lavers, RNLI lifeboat from Aldeburgh. Taken to Dunkirk by Sub Lt T Betts, RNVR.

Mary Scott, RNLI lifeboat stationed at Southwold. Responsible for ferrying troops off the beaches from May 30. Abandoned after suffering engine trouble, but returned after repairs.

Louise Stephens, RNLI lifeboat stationed at Great Yarmouth. Rescued over 40 men.

Guide of Dunkirk, RNLI lifeboat originally intended for Clacton-on-Sea but impounded by the Admiralty straight from the yard at Rowhedge on June 1 to participate in the evacuation. Manned by volunteers from Frinton and Walton, she fell victim to machine-gun fire and had to be towed back to England stern first after fouling her propeller. During her return trip to France, she was damaged by shell fire. Although only listed as Lifeboat no 826, she was named *Guide of Dunkirk* in 1947 in honour of the Girl Guides Association who had raised funds during various war charity appeals.

Michael Stephens, RNLI lifeboat from Lowestoft, stationed at Dunkirk.

EMED, RNLI lifeboat stationed at Walton-on-the-Naze. Built in 1928, this 48 ft long, sail-assisted boat went to Dunkirk, surviving strafing raids which took several of the small boats she was towing at the time. The naval officer in charge, Lt Mead was killed by an exploding shell. The boat was later found by the tug *Sun IV* and towed safely back to Dover with her complement of 39 men.

Greater London, RNLI lifeboat stationed at Southend. Played an important part during the latter stages of the evacuation, transferring several hundred stranded soldiers to ships lying in deeper water.

Edward Z Dresden, RNLI lifeboat stationed at Clacton-on-Sea used to transfer men from the quays and wharfs to ships standing off in deep water. She was one of the last vessels to return from Dunkirk, towing a lifeboat full of wounded men.

Watchful, HM Tender, originally commissioned as a pleasure boat under the name *Brit II*, trading around the Norfolk coast. Converted to a base ship for the navy to carry arms and stores to destroyers lying off Yarmouth. During the Dunkirk evacuation, she helped to rescue nearly 1000 stranded servicemen from the beaches.

Dab II, motor yacht built at Lowestoft in 1931, commandeered by the navy for the Dunkirk crisis. She had been berthed at Heybridge on the

Blackwater when taken over by Lt R W Thompson, RNVR who made three trips across the Channel.

Singapore II, Ipswich-based 32 ft motor cruiser built at Walton-on-the-Naze in 1937. Taken to Dunkirk by Sub Lt F E Greenfell.

East Anglians were to see many more naval engagements before the end of the war. With its long, difficult to defend coastline, East Anglia was vulnerable to attack from the sea. Beaches and cliffs were heavily defended and men of the National Defence Corps, a specially trained band of mainly ex-servicemen guarded naval oil storage tanks and pipelines at Felixstowe, Ipswich and Harwich against sabotage attempts.

The navy commandeered the piers at Southend just a few days before war was declared. Southend became HQ for Thames and Medway control and was the main assembly point for east coast convoys. Masters used the pier as a briefing point. During the war years, 3367 convoys consisting of 34,297 ships rendezvoused there. A giant boom was built between Shoeburyness and the Kent coast to prevent attack from enemy submarines or motor torpedo boats.

One of the first major losses of the war was the sinking of the Dutch passenger ship *Simon Bolivar*. On Saturday November 18, 1939, this 8300 ton liner was bound for Paramaribo in Dutch Guinea (now Surinam) with 93 first class passengers plus 134 officers and men. The last word in floating luxury, she could travel at 14 1/2 knots and was 420 ft long.

Trevor King, Essex writer and researcher has spent over 25 years investigating the loss of the *Simon Bolivar*. One of his contacts, Stanley Day, actually saw the disaster. Mr Day was working at sea, about 15 miles south of Harwich in an area known as The Sunk, when he saw the ship in the distance and identified her as the *Simon Bolivar*.

"I understand her captain was seeking a pilot" he recalled. "None was available, so the *Simon Bolivar* continued her passage down the Kentish Knock Channel, intending no doubt to pick up a Thames pilot further on. She had only steamed for about half a mile when there was a terrific explosion. It shook our own vessel. Obviously, the ship had hit a mine."

"Two RN vessels started picking up the survivors who were drenched in fuel oil. The ship had exploded amidships in about eight to ten fathoms of water. Only the funnels remained visible."

Trevor King takes up the story:

"Despite Holland's neutral stance, *Simon Bolivar's* master, Captain H Voorspuiy, a highly respected senior officer in the Dutch merchant fleet was aware of the festering hostility in the North Sea. The war was less than three months old, but even then, neutral flags were merely an academic pretence in shipping lanes polluted by sophisticated mines attached with mechanisms calibrated to destroy vessels of any nationality – enemy or otherwise."

*The wreck of the destroyer **Gipsy** lost off Harwich when she was struck by a mine.*

Wrens stationed at Point Clea manned installations at the nearby Brightlingsea minesweeper base.

As the ship headed for the open sea, Dutch sources claim her fate was already sealed. That same night, three German aircraft deposited a cluster of Hitler's secret weapon, the deadly magnetic mine, in the area of The Sunk. However, Harwich veterans will tell you that Nazi seaplanes and submarines – and even a few neutral ships – were suspected of actively mining the Harwich approaches long before the *Simon Bolivar* loss."

"At approximately 11.30 am, Captain Voorspuiy stood close to the helm, his Third Officer, A P Praamsma a little way off, as his ship steamed down the Knock Channel. Below the bridge, passengers relaxed in the smoking lounge with the Purser. Suddenly, a resounding explosion occurred amidships, as the *Simon Bolivar* activated a magnetic mine. Captain Voorspuiy was wounded and died soon after. Third Officer Praamsma lay seriously injured; Purser Coster and the passengers in the smoking lounge died immediately."

"Fractured fuel tanks and pipes spilled oil into the sea. Above, the ten lifeboats were being lowered by their davits, but the vessel's rapid sinking by the stern made the task difficult. With her masts destroyed and radio damaged, an SOS could not be broadcast."

"Fifteen minutes or so later a second explosion shook the ship, accelerating her end, and increasing the casualty toll alarmingly. The second explosion was directly underneath a fully-laden lifeboat in the throes of being lowered down the ship's side, pitching the occupants into a morass of oil and sea. The oil began to ignite, and many perished, including babies and young children. Relatives and friends were abruptly parted, some never to be reunited. Yet, remarkably, according to Dutch accounts, there was little or no panic."

The late T H Bernard, a well-known East Anglian clothing manufacturer was Area Civil Defence Controller at the time. His diary entry for November 18 reads:

'At 7 pm, I was telephoned to take some clothing to Parkeston Quay for survivors. Filled the car with clothing and proceeded to the hotel on the Quay. It was a dirty night. The survivors, men, women and children, Dutch and natives, 260 in number, 40 stretcher cases. It was a pitiful and distressing sight. The passengers were covered in fuel oil. We started to issue clothing when I had to leave for the Report Centre because of an air raid warning.'

'I later received a message that the survivors had been hurried on to the London train. A mother thought she had lost her child, but the following day, at the Cottage Hospital, a baby which was so discoloured that it was thought to be black, was found after being cleaned to be white. The mother was in Colchester Hospital – well, guess her feelings.'

Howard Bell, then aged 17, now RNLI honorary liaison officer for the Eastern region was also at Parkeston Quay as the survivors arrived.

He remembers helping the WRVS members to distribute clothing, blankets, hot drinks and food to the survivors. Many were suffering from the effects of shock as they disembarked from naval and harbour craft. Many were also covered in thick oil.

HELP to clear the Seas of the Enemy—

—with the Aid of Your Savings!

Hitler is all out to cut our life-line. But this NEVER WILL happen if you throw your whole weight now into the Battle. Our Merchant Navy must be free to bring us vital supplies of food and war materials. Save and Lend every shilling you can. Back up our Ships with your savings. Save and Lend to-day and every day—to build an ever mightier Navy

Meanwhile, the injured were being ferried to Harwich and District Hospital, Essex County Hospital in Colchester and the East Suffolk Hospital at Ipswich. Two crew members were admitted to Shotley naval barracks with serious injuries.

At Essex County Hospital, the arrival of 13 survivors coincided with an air raid alert. While ambulance crews were transferring the patients to the wards, local police were sent to investigate the reasons for lights being shown during an alert. Some victims needed immediate surgery, and theatre staff worked far into Sunday without rest.

Even amid such scenes of tragedy and confusion, there was some light relief. One survivor, Walter Busby, was so caked in thick fuel oil it was impossible to distinguish his sex. Nursing staff, after listening to his rather high-pitched voice, decided he was female and wheeled him into a women's ward. Here he stayed until the following day when an application of petrol and hot water revealed his true identity.

Howard Bell, the teenager who helped at Parkeston Quay recalls the story of baby Simon.

"I was not to know at the time, but my future wife was involved. Her mother was a patient in Harwich and District Hospital where some of the survivors had been taken. Among them was a baby that no one could identify – most likely its parents had been drowned. My wife's mother comforted the baby since he had no name, she called him Simon after the ship. Later, the Dutch authorities in London accepted responsibility for him. If only we knew what became of him. He would be about 51 now."

Simon was, in fact, West Indian.

Among the ship's passengers were several nuns and Dutch Sisters of

Mercy. Soon after the ship was crippled, the Harwich-bound ferry spotted movement on *Simon Bolivar's* poop deck. Pulling alongside, the ferry rescued a Dutch Sister of Mercy who promptly passed over a box containing two small children covered in black oil.

The magnetic mine was to claim many other victims in the North Sea. *Terukuni Maru*, a 12,000 ton Japanese liner was sunk just off Harwich on November 21 1939. Crowds of spectators lined the seafront to watch the rescue operation. Fortunately, there was no loss of life but many injuries.

A lot of enemy activity was reported that Tuesday. At about 9.23 pm a Heinkel 115 seaplane was heard approaching *HMS Badger* (the Harwich naval base), and dropped what later turned out to be a magnetic mine. After machine-gunning the area, the plane flew off.

A patrol of three destroyers from the First Destroyer Flotilla based at Harwich, *HMS Gipsy* (H63), *HMS Boadicea* (H65) and the Polish *Burza* set off in the inky blackness of the unlit harbour to investigate the disturbance. Just inside Landguard Point, *Gipsy* hit the mine and was ripped apart. She sank within minutes and 30 sailors including the captain died. Many people rushed to the seafront to help, but the barbed wire and other defences made it impossible to get near to the drowning men. Special Constable Leslie Petch, who had been on patrol along the seafront, recalls seeing searchlights playing about the icy waters as small craft rescued survivors. "I was so close to them, I felt as though I could just reach out my hand and pluck them to safety, but barbed wire defences and steep harbour walls spelt out the futility of such action."

Another early wartime loss was *Ocean Lassie*, an examination vessel which went to the bottom within a minute of being struck by a parachute mine. Only six survived from the original crew of 13.

Defending the coastline meant that holes had to be blown in piers and jetties – which caused problems for lifeboat crews attempting to rescue survivors from stricken ships. In many cases, the lifeboat crew was cut off from the boat and equipment. At Clacton, a hole was blown in the pier without notice, leaving the lifeboat *Edward Z Dresden* stranded in her boathouse at the other end. Extensive damage was caused to both boat and equipment, and she had to be taken to Rowhedge for repairs. Later, she operated from Brightlingsea until the gap in the pier was bridged.

The RNLI played a key role in the war at sea. Between September 1939 and April 1940, 135 British ships and 143 neutrals were sunk around the British coast. During the first nine months of war, Britain's lifeboats were launched 315 times. As the Phoney War gave way to the real thing, boats were launched 370 times in 12 weeks, helping to save 895 shipwrecked souls and 39 vessels. The first wartime lifeboat call-out was answered by the Aldeburgh No. 1 boat, which went to the rescue of the 8640 ton liner *Magdapur* sunk off the Suffolk coast during the first week of the war. Crew

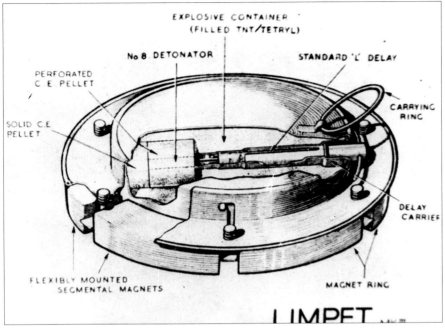

EXPLOSIVE CONTAINER
(FILLED TNT/TETRYL)

No 8 DETONATOR

STANDARD 'L' DELAY

PERFORATED
C E PELLET

CARRYING
RING

SOLID C.E.
PELLET

DELAY
CARRIER

FLEXIBLY MOUNTED
SEGMENTAL MAGNETS

MAGNET RING

LIMPET

Top: *The dreaded Limpet mine.*

Above: *Colonel R S Macrae, inventor of the Limpet.*

Left: *Seaman Gunner C J Singleton testing a 20 mm Oerlikon gun aboard an American lease-lend mine-sweeper. These ships were brought from the USA by men stationed at Lowestoft.*

members saved 18 Europeans and 56 Lascars. Six men were lost and they say it took 18 hours to clean the congealed blood and oil from the lifeboat.

Lifeboat call-outs weren't easy. Boats were launched without floodlights and in the early days of the war, even the use of wireless was forbidden in case of listening submarines. Maroons couldn't be used, so crew members were summoned by bicycle messengers.

Sometimes, several boats were called out to the same incident. Such was the case on August 6, 1941, when six ships from a passing convoy ran aground on Happisburgh sandbanks. The navy called on Cromer, Gorleston, Lowestoft and Sheringham boats to assist. Great Yarmouth assisted in the actual rescue, but Sheringham (20 miles away) and Lowestoft (25 miles away) arrived too late. It took three hours to rescue 119 men.

As enemy activity was stepped up, the stretch of water between Happisburgh Sands and the Norfolk coast became known as, 'E-Boat Alley.' It was here that fast German E-boats would lurk, waiting to pounce on slow moving convoys. Men of the RNLI answered distress calls to this area defended with a couple of service rifles and 50 rounds of ammunition – a terrible risk. It is recorded that the only time this armament was used in anger was to explode runaway sea mines.

As well as rescue, lifeboats helped with coastal defences. Certain members of the Clacton boat helped the War Office in secret experiments. In 1943, Cox Charles Ellis and Commander Tansley set out to sea with Dr A Klein, a Jewish refugee who had escaped from Austria. Dr Klein's invention was to save the lives of many ditched airmen, for armed with his tiny still, they could distil seawater for drinking.

During the Battle of Britain, the lifeboats rescued both Allied and enemy airmen. The Walton and Frinton boat, *EMED* was called out five times in 1940 and seven in 1941 to crashed aircraft. In one incident, they found a dead German pilot floating upright supported by his lifejacket. The landlord of a seafront public house in Sheringham spotted a dark speck out to sea. When the lifeboat got there, it turned out to be five Polish airmen, afloat without food for 17 hours.

With the introduction of the Second Front and the invasion of Europe in 1944, and with transport and glider forces being built up, more than 75 per cent of disaster calls answered by Anglian lifeboats involved aircrews and aircraft. The boats worked in close harmony with Air Sea Rescue stationed at Gorleston. During the latter stages of the war, this force had the task of tracking and rescuing airborne lifeboats which were carried beneath the fuselage of specially adapted aircraft and were dropped to men drifting in rubber dinghies. These boats were fitted with small petrol engines, sails, a radio and a store of supplies.

Clearing magnetic mines was vital if shipping was to keep moving. When mines were dropped by parachute into the Thames and Harwich Harbour in

1939, magnetic sweeping was introduced. This took the form of a 40 ft long wooden skid which was pulled behind a ship. A heavy electric cable was wound around pegs. This cable was linked to a generator on the ship. The role of the generator was to keep a surge of power passing through the cable to clear the mines. Several of these sweeps were built at Wivenhoe shipyard. Wooden mine sweepers were also built there. These sturdy ships, similar to a Yarmouth drifter, pulled a double longitudinal sweep through which a surge of current was passed, causing the mines to explode. A pulse of 3000 amps went through the cables every minute - enough to explode all the mines on the sea bottom over an area of about ten acres.

Skids were later replaced by de-gaussing coils which were wrapped around the hull above the water line. These de-magnetised the mines, leaving them harmless. By the end of May 1940, 2000 merchant ships and 1704 warships had been fitted with de-gaussing coils.

The chance to examine the innards of a magnetic mine came when one fell into tidal water off Shoeburyness. Lt Cdr Ouvry of *HMS Vernon* and Dr A B Wood of the Naval Mine Design Department had the mine dragged to shore at low water. Another one was found nearby on the same day. Using non-magnetic brass tools the mines were dismantled and analysed. Among one of the few men to work on magnetic mines in the field was Lionel Hawkins RNVR – a descendant of Hawkins of Elizabethan fame. He, together with his assistant Mr G Goss, was killed while examining a mine which exploded at Walton-on-the-Naze.

ANGLIAN DAILY TIMES, THURSDAY, NOVEMBER

BRITISH DESTROYER HITS MINE OFF EAST COAST

FORTY RATINGS MISSING : TWENTY-ONE MEN INJURED

SHORE CROWDS WATCH RESCUE DRAMA

SIX GERMAN 'PLANES RAID SHETLANDS : SEAPLANE HIT

ENEMY MACHINE IN THRILLING CHASE OVER THAMES AREA

IT WAS OFFICIALLY STATED BY THE ADMIRALTY LAST NIGHT THAT THE DESTROYER GIPSY STRUCK A MINE OFF THE EAST COAST ON TUESDAY AND WAS BEACHED.

TWENTY-ONE OFFICERS AND MEN WERE INJURED. AND FORTY RATINGS ARE REPORTED TO BE MISSING.

Many people on shore heard the explosion, and saw the rescue of the destroyer's crew as searchlights lit up the scene.

Six German warplanes yesterday carried out a daring bombing raid on the Shetland Islands.

An attempt to attack shipping failed, the raiders being beaten off by gunfire, but they then bombed an R.A.F. seaplane at its moorings and set it on fire. Flying so low that their crews could be seen they dropped a rain of bombs.

There were no British casualties.

There was also German air activity in the South-East, and British fighters engaged one raider in a fierce combat over the Thames. Guns were in action both in the morning and afternoon, and reports indicated that more than one Nazi warplane had crossed the coast.

LAST NIGHT'S AIR ALARMS : RAIDER SHOT DOWN

An air raid warning sounded in a town in Essex last night. The 'all clear" was given half-an-hour later.

Air M... ... ann... ...hat one enemy aircraft was sh... l...

The fishing industry suffered badly from mines, machine-gun and bombing raids - and from the many restrictions introduced for security reasons. One popular yarn around Brightlingsea relates how, during the early part of the war when boats were not allowed out past a certain point, one boat on an illicit trip trawled up a half-decomposed body full of eels. Removing the fish, one of the crew asked what they should do with the body. "Chuck 'im back" was the reply. The next night, the men returned to haul in the float-marked corpse, again full of eels. This was to go on for several nights until wind and tide changed, sweeping the remains into deeper water.

At Lowestoft, a major AA battery was established to protect the town and coast. Two batteries were sited on College Farm and Pakefield golf course. During the war, Lowestoft was an important naval shipbuilding and operational base. *HMS Europa*, HQ for the Royal Naval Patrol Service, was located in the Sparrow's Nest Theatre. The town was surrounded by pillboxes, trenches and barbed wire entanglements. The Claremont Pier was blown in half to halt invaders and additional weapons were positioned on the seafront.

With the ever-present threat of sneak hit-and-run attacks from German naval forces, the dock basin at Felixstowe became the first operational motor torpedo base in January 1940, under the command of Lt Cdr C M Donner. Bases were named after stinging insects because of their ability to carry out fast attacks on the enemy. Felixstowe was *HMS Beehive*, Great Yarmouth *HMS Mantis* and Lowestoft *HMS Midge*.

There was very little protection aboard the powerful, fast MTB's. Built of thin plywood, boats were armed with two torpedoes and light machine-guns. The 16-man crew worked in cramped conditions alongside 4000 gallons of high-octane fuel. There was very little chance of survival if the boat received a direct hit.

WRNS played an important part in looking after MTB crews. They serviced guns, ammunition and torpedoes, and supplied coffee, sandwiches and thermos flasks of soup.

Felixstowe MTB's were in a major battle on October 1, 1944, while carrying out attacks on enemy convoys off the Dutch coast. During this action, a number of craft were raked with machine-gun fire and MTB 347 was lost with little hope of survivors.

CHAPTER EIGHT

Death from the Air

*T*he Phoney War came to an abrupt end in East Anglia on April 30, 1940. An HE 111H-4 of the 1st Staffel of Kampfgruppe 126, (a coastal unit specialising in minelaying around the East Anglian coast), had been above the region intent on sowing the two parachute mines suspended on external racks beneath the aircraft. Things went wrong when a thick blanket of fog descended.

The pilot, 25 year old Oberleutnant und Flugzeugfuhrer Hermann Vagts flew blind until, at about 11.15 pm, he broke cover near the Bawdsey radar station. AA batteries around the coast were put on alert, and guns opened up as the plane flew off towards Felixstowe. The Harwich battery also opened fire and it is believed that shells bursting close to the Heinkel caused extensive damage to the engine and rudder mechanism. Flying in ever-decreasing circles, the pilot found himself over Clacton. 'Jeff' Jeffries, a wartime member of the fire brigade saw the plane approaching.

"At the station, we heard the sound of low flying aircraft, and by the strange noises she was making, reckoned something was wrong. She came overhead, circled the town, headed out to sea, then turned towards Holland-on-Sea and came down low over the recreation ground as if trying to land."

If the pilot had indeed been trying to land, then things went wrong. Approaching from the sea, the Heinkel, now losing altitude, with one engine out and the other misfiring, skimmed the rooftops, knocking off several chimney pots before bouncing over a lamp standard to hit the side of 25 Victoria Road, Clacton, home of Mr & Mrs Frederick Gill and their 19-year-old son William.

Eye witness accounts stress that at least two flares had been fired from the plane as if to warn those below as it circled the area with flames flickering around the engine and fuselage.

Once the sound of rending metal stopped, a strange silence seemed to hang over the smoking wreck. Some thought there was an interval of only seconds, while others say it was a few minutes before, without warning, the whole area was devastated by an ear-bursting, earth-shattering explosion as one of the two C-type parachute mines ignited. Machine-gun cartridges exploded – to the imminent danger of anyone in the area.

People who had been running towards the scene of the crash were picked up bodily by the blast. Others, standing close to windows had their faces and bodies slashed by flying glass.

That evening, Detective Sergeant E J Barkway and an inspector were on duty at Clacton police station with a night duty clerk. Unaware of the actual cause of the explosion, the police alerted all available personnel with Boy Scouts acting as runners and messengers.

Although fire, police and ARP organisations had been practising for such an event since 1938, the professionalism of the forces attending the disaster surprised even the authorities.

Roads and avenues around the crash site were littered with debris. Tall trees were split and scorched; garden shrubs were denuded of leaves and blossom.

Jeff Jeffries heard the explosion as he and the fire brigade were on their way to the crash site.

"When we eventually arrived, just a few minutes later, it was a terrible sight. The spot where Mr & Mrs Gill's house had stood was completely flattened, with only a great pile of bricks and rubble left. What was left of the plane had been tossed against the wall of a nearby house, the wings torn off and lying to one side. About 20 yards away, we found the bodies of the four German airmen, all black and burned."

Those in the vicinity did what they could to help the wounded and bewildered homeless. One of the first on the scene was Freddie Venn, who had been out driving with his fiancee. Stumbling among the pile of rubble which had once been the Gill's home and hearing a cry for help, he eventually found an apparently disembodied hand waving from a pile of masonry. The victim was young William Gill. Mr Venn held his hand until the Heavy Rescue Team arrived to free the badly injured lad.

Cameramen and reporters flocked to the area. Ironically, local newspapers respected existing Government restrictions on publication of photographs of the damage - the nationals had no such scruples. One enterprising local photographer secretly snapped the damage. One of these pictures found its way into a German-orientated newspaper and was studied closely by Third Reich bomb experts so they could make any necessary adjustments to the mine which they planned to use in future night bombing raids on Britain.

During the night and much of the following morning, firemen, rescue teams and police beavered away to clear the debris and re-settle the homeless. Unknown to these workers, the second mine had not exploded and was lying in the garden, surrounded by debris. Several visitors to the

Raymond Baxter (second from left) plans a V-rocket site raid with comrades from RAF Coltishall.

area used it as a makeshift seat. Even DS Barkway recalls resting his foot on it several times, thinking that it was the hot water tank from the damaged house. Later examination showed that the so-called water tank had no inlet or outlet pipes and was stencilled with instructions in a foreign language. Realisation struck and the whole area was evacuated.

Lt Cdr R J H Ryan and CPO R V Ellingworth from *HMS Vernon* were called in to deal with the mine. With more luck than judgement (it was established later that the mine could have been fitted with anti-tamper devices), they made it safe. It was then loaded on to a truck, loaned by Bryan's Garage of Old Road, Clacton, and driven by Frank Leatherdale to Portsmouth for further inspection. Both naval officers were later killed attempting to de-fuse a parachute mine hanging from a warehouse roof in Dagenham and were awarded the posthumous George Cross.

It was decided that the four German airmen should be buried with full military honours. On Saturday May 4, crowds lined the streets as RAF lorries carrying the swastika-draped coffins drove through the town to the graveyard at Burrsville. Extra police had been drafted in as a precaution against demonstrations, but despite an outcry from some of the popular press, the airmen were laid to rest amid floral tributes from local people and RAF stations. The coffins were lowered to a volley of shots from the honour party. The German airmen killed were Hermann Vagts, aged 25, Hermann Sodtmann, 24, Karl-Heinz Fresen, 26 and Hans-Gunther Koch, 21.

For some days after the crash, the area swarmed with staff officers and Air Ministry technicians searching the wreckage for information. Unfortunately, souvenir hunters had made off with most of the more interesting items. Former regular fireman, the late Reg Lawes found a leather belt with a swastika and eagle buckle. "It had the name 'Fresen' written on the inside," he recalled.

On Monday May 11, Mr & Mrs Gill were buried. Their funeral was attended by local officials and various volunteer organisations. The grave is unmarked, but a seat opposite the site of their home records that the Gills were Britain's first civilian casualties. Soon after, death from the air became an everyday fear for the people of East Anglia.

May 10 marked the escalation of the war with blitzkrieg attacks on Belgium, Holland and Luxembourg. The German high command had drawn up plans under the code name Nord-West for the invasion of England with a major landing aimed at East Anglia. The War Diary records events in those tense times:

Friday 10 May, 1940
Enemy aircraft activity caused the following Districts to be under yellow warnings at various times between 0350 and 0504 hours: King's Lynn, Colchester, Ipswich, Chelmsford.

There has been some activity on the part of enemy aircraft off the south east coast and Thames estuary. No bombs were dropped, but slight damage was done to the roofs of bungalows at Canvey Island by falling fragments of anti-aircraft shells.

Saturday, 11 May
No important enemy action reported. An unidentified aeroplane was seen flying north to south over Harwich. Anti-aircraft guns fired about eight rounds. The aeroplane, which showed a tail light was seen to pass out to sea between Clacton and Walton. No bombs were dropped.

Sunday, 12 May
Certain districts in East Anglia were under yellow warning at various times between 2134 and 2203 hours. Rumours of parachute landings in East Anglia were current last night. They seem to have their origin in bursts of anti-aircraft shells near Marham.

Sunday, 13 May
No enemy action has been reported, Unsubstantiated rumours of parachutists in south east England continue to be current.

Tuesday, 14 May

No enemy action reported. Cambridge Region report further landing of refugees at an east coast port this afternoon.

Wednesday, 22 May

There was enemy activity over East Anglia and Kent. A few bombs were dropped and a British plane was brought down by AA fire at Rainham. No serious damage to property has been reported, but two persons were slightly injured by broken window glass. The pilot, the only occupant of the plane, escaped by parachute.

Saturday, 25 May

A bomb fell at Langley near Loddon, Norfolk, at 0125. Two cottages damaged and a cow and a pony killed. A second bomb fell at Wickford at 0155. Chicken houses were damaged.

Sunday, 2 June

The following districts were under yellow warning last night: King's Lynn, Bury St Edmunds, Boston, Lincoln. These were due to returning British aeroplanes, one of which dropped two HE bombs near a searchlight site at Strumpshaw, wounding one man and damaging telegraph wires.

What do I do...

if I find bombs, mines or bits of aircraft?

I DO NOT TOUCH THEM, but report them immediately to the police.

I remember that lives have been lost through tampering with objects which contain explosives.

I remember too that even things which may not be explosive often provide the authorities with information which may be very important.

Cut this out — and keep it!

Issued by The Ministry of Information
Space presented to the Nation by the Brewers' Society

Tuesday, 4 June

A barrage balloon at Harwich was hit by British aircraft at 0250; the cable fell in the street and the aircraft crashed. Yellow warnings were given at various times in Canterbury, Colchester, Ipswich and Norwich.

Saturday, 8 June

At 2230, a Heinkel minelayer crashed and exploded near Woodbridge, East Suffolk. Two of the crew were killed and one badly injured taken to hospital under guard. Eyke Old Rectory was considerably damaged and windows broken in the police station.

Thursday, 13 June

At 0235, a British bomber fouled the balloon barrage at Harwich and crashed into the dock area at Felixstowe, causing a fire in the store at Marriages mill. There was no trace of the crew who are believed to have been burned.

The above was a Hampden bomber (P4345) of 144 Squadron based at Waddington. Coming within range of the guns at Harwich, which opened fire, the aircraft dropped red and green recognition flares. Obviously in serious trouble, the plane fouled the barrage balloon cable and crashed into the flour mill, setting it on fire. The barges *Golden Grain*, *Phoenician*, *The Miller* and *Rayjohn* plus five railway trucks were also burnt. Mr D Grayling, working nearby, died of his injuries.

Bodies of the aircrew were found later. The men were Wing Commander Joseph Watts, Pilot Officer John Andrews, Sgt Ronald Jolly, DFM and Sgt Alexander Winstanley.

Things were looking so serious at this time in the war, that the Government actually considered using poison gas against the enemy. On June 15, 1940, two days after the fall of Dunkirk, the Chief of Imperial Staff, Sir John Dill, gave details of a gas scheme to military chiefs. The following memo (War office file, WO 193/732) has been restricted information for the past 30 years.

'There are strong military arguments in favour of such action. Enemy forces crowded on the beaches, with the confusion inevitable on first landing, would present a splendid target. Gas spray by aircraft under such conditions would be likely to have a more widespread and wholesale effect than high explosives. It can, moreover, be applied very rapidly, and is particularly suitable in an operation where we may get very little warning ....

...... Besides gas spray, contamination of beaches, obstacles and defiles by liquid mustard would have a great delaying effect. The use of gas in general would have the effect of slowing up operations, and we believe that speed must be the essence of any successful invasion of this country. There are, of course, grave objections to taking this step ....'

Despite condemnation from several of Dill's staff, Churchill was in agreement and wrote:

'Let me have a report on the amount of mustard or other variants we have in store, and whether it can be used in air bombs as well as fired from guns. What is our output per month? It should certainly be speeded up. Let me have proposals. Supposing lodgements were effected on our coast, there could be no better points for the application of mustard than these beaches and lodgements. In my view, there would be no need to wait for the enemy to adopt such methods. He will certainly adopt them if he thinks it will pay. Home Defence should be consulted as to whether prompt drenching of lodgements would not be a great help. Everything should be brought to the highest pitch of readiness, but the question of actual employment must be settled by the cabinet.'

The scheme was suicidal. Britain only had 450 tons of mustard gas. Everything would have been staked on just one day. Bomber Command could ferry enough poison gas to spray a strip 60 yards wide and 400 miles long, but then stocks would be exhausted, leaving the Germans to deploy their own chemical warfare units unhindered.

The period that followed, covering the months from July to September 1940, has gone down in our history as the Battle of Britain. With German forces massing on the French coast, ready for invasion, the authorities found themselves desperately short of air support – especially as many planes were lost at Dunkirk. Part of the German invasion plan was that the Luftwaffe should soften up British defences before the main force moved in. It was this softening up process that became known as the Battle of Britain.

The protection of East Anglia lay with 11 Group, made up at the beginning of the battle by the following stations:

65 and 75 Squadrons, Spitfires, Hornchurch.
54 Squadron, Spitfires, Rochford.
56 and 151 Squadrons, Hurricanes, North Weald.
25 Squadron, Blenheims, Martlesham Heath.
85 Squadron, Hurricanes, Martlesham Heath.
264 Squadron, Defiants, Duxford.
17 Squadron, Hurricanes, Debden.
66 Squadron, Spitfires, Coltishall.
242 Squadron, Hurricanes, Coltishall.

July 11 is generally reckoned to be the day the battle began over East Anglia, when Squadron Leader Peter Townsend, flying Hurricane P2716: VY-F of 85 Squadron was shot down by a Do 17 off Harwich. Another Dornier fell victim to the guns of Squadron Leader Douglas Bader of 242 Squadron off Cromer, yet another was badly damaged by fighters of 66 Squadron off Yarmouth.

On July 12, the southbound convoy *Booty* came under heavy attack while steaming off the coast. During this action, Heinkel He 111H-2 8/KG53 was shot down by Pilot Officer K Manger and Flt Sgt G Griffiths, 10 miles NNW of Aldeburgh light. Another Heinkel, He 111H-2 111/KG53 was shot down by Pilot Officer G E Pittmann and Sgt D Fopp of 17 Squadron and crashed into the sea off Orfordness. The observer from this plane, Helmut von Brocke was rescued but died shortly afterwards. He was buried at sea near the South West Bawdsey buoy.

Norwich suffered its first attack by enemy fire on the afternoon of July 9, a few days before the battle proper really started. Without warning, two low-flying aircraft screamed in over the city to attack Boulton & Paul. Ten workers were killed and 68 injured. The nearby LNER loco sheds were badly damaged. Colman's Carrow Road factory suffered 20 casualties and two workers were killed when bombs were dropped on Barnard's at Mousehold.

August 15 was another hectic day for the region. Nearly 40 dive-bombers with fighter escorts sneaked in through the defences over Suffolk and Essex to attack the base at Martlesham Heath. On that day, the Luftwaffe lost 75 aircraft during the battle, 15 were lost returning to base, and three downed in accidents.

By now, Fighter Command could muster 672 aircraft, including six Blenheim and two Defiant Squadrons and a flight of Gladiators. Trained pilots were still thin on the ground; at least 350 new pilots were needed to bring Squadrons up to strength - and there were only 75 in the pipeline. To overcome this shortage, the Air Ministry suggested that fighter operational training units should concentrate on processing Czech, Polish and other Allied volunteers who would form their own national squadrons. These men were to be passed out as battle ready after a two week crash course of 14–20 hours flying.

Losses during the early part of August were grave; 94 pilots were killed or missing, 60 injured, 175 planes lost, 65 needing repair and 30 damaged on bases.

Plane crashes became part of everyday life – as this incident report from Chelmsford police shows. Sadly, many of these reports were inaccurate on locations and aircraft type.

August 31, 1940
Hawker Hurricane IP 3383 Fg. O M C Doulton, 61 Sq. Debden Cat. 3. Missing. Shot down by Messerchmitts and crashed into the River Colne off Aldboro Point. Pilot killed previous to crash. Plane buried in mud and non-recoverable.

Junkers Ju 88 shot down and crashed into mud flats off East Mersea gun position near Mersea Stone. Plane wrecked.

Unidentified aircraft (believed Ju 88) shot down and crashed into mouth of River Colne, Plane lost. Fate of crew not known.

Heinkel He 111 shot down and destroyed by fire at point 880 yds SE of Hill Farm, Layer near Abbeton. 111 KG 53 Legion Condor Lille-Nord Codes A1 - Oblt Huhn, Gefr Erwin Gleissner and two other unknown killed. One taken POW. Time, 1604 hrs.

Messerschmitt Bf 110 shot down and destroyed at Flories Farm, Great Tey. Plane exploded, crew killed. Time, 1625 hours.

2 October, 1940
Junkers Ju 88 shot down during the night and crashed on to the rear of the sewage works at Brightlingsea. Plane partially damaged, crew captured. Time, 0200 hours.

29 October, 1940
Messerschmitt Bf 109 shot down and crashed at Langenhoe Lodge near Langenhoe. Pilot captured unhurt. Time, approx 1600 hours.

Often, wartime official records are quite different from reality – as in the case of an Me 100 shot down over Smith's Sandpits, Clacton during a dogfight on August 18.

Just after tea, a flight of enemy aircraft was seen approaching from the east. Hubert Page of Great Clacton was home on leave and recalls the scene.

"I remember my mother called me out into the garden to see what she thought was a swarm of bees hovering above our apple tree. Instead of bees, I saw nearly 100 German planes, flying so high that there were white exhaust trails. Next thing I saw was six or seven British fighters – no more, that's for sure – first over the rooftops then, right up among the Jerries. They scattered all over the place, with a lot of bombers making towards the south. The others stayed to fight, and the whole sky was taken up with diving, wheeling, fighting aircraft."

One of the planes, a Me 110 was hit and came wheeling down, closely followed by a British fighter. Engines screaming, the stricken plane dived into the centre of the town. Patrol officer Frederick Wolton was on the first fire engine to arrive at the scene.

"I shall always remember that dreadful scream of engines as the Me 110 dived. At the time, I thought the plane was coming straight for us. After the sound of the crash, our thoughts were for the poor devils that must surely be trapped in houses in the area. It came as something of a shock when we did at last find the spot ..... nothing damaged, not even a plane of glass broken. There was no sign of the plane, just a hole in the ground and a heap of wet sand slowly sliding back into the pond. There were a few small fires in the surrounding bushes and a few pieces of shattered aluminium ...."

PO Wolton may well have been one of the first official visitors to the scene – but 13-year-old George Watton was quicker. Smith's Sandpits, worked out, wild and overgrown, was a mecca for the local children, and one of George's favourite haunts. His mother kept chickens on allotments nearby and he was preparing chicken feed when the Me crashed.

"We stood by the pens measuring out the grain when we heard this terrible screaming noise" he explained. "I knew it was a plane in trouble and as the noise got louder and closer, I grabbed Ma and threw her to the ground for safety. I honestly thought the thing was going to land on top of us, so close did it come. I was half expecting an almighty bang, but there was just a dull whumph sound. I ran across the footpath, through the hedge and down to the first pit. I remember feeling things dropping down on me as I ran – mud, stones and wet sand. When I got there, I was just in time to see mud and sand sliding back into a deep hole. Several small fires had started among the bushes, and there were bits of greeny-blue leather lying around. I grabbed some and ran off home before anyone saw me. Years later, in the 1970s, I was digging on the allotments and came across a length of burnt and twisted aluminium tubing and a piece from a flyer's headphone set."

Police and RAF authorities searched the area and even put feeler rods into the pond, but were unable to find the plane. Luftwaffe records for that period list only three missing aircraft fitting the Me's description – but a further clue emerged in the 1960s when I was shown a model Me bearing a tag with the number and identification of the downed aircraft. After the crash, the area was sealed off and patrolled by Specials and Wardens. Special Constable W A Rampling, on patrol, chanced to stumble on a small fragment of aluminium bearing the plane's identification details. He took it home to make a memento of his part in the crash.

The pilot who shot down the Me was Pilot Officer (later Group Captain) Colin F Gray, DFC, DSO, serving with the New Zealand Air Force based in East Anglia with RAF 54 Squadron. This is his account of the Smith's Sandpit incident.

"This aircraft pulled up vertically in front of me as I fired, and I have always assumed that the pilot and rear gunner must have been killed because it appeared to do a wing-over and dive straight down into the middle of Clacton-on-Sea. The Me 110 was travelling very fast in the dive, and although I attempted to follow initially, I soon gave this up as a bad job and watched it spiral down all the way until it crashed. I certainly did not see anyone bail out."

Colin Gray survived the war and became a successful businessman at home in New Zealand. He returned to England for a visit in the 70s and took

Victoria Road, Clacton, the site of Britain's first civilian fatalities.

Norwich was badly hit during the Baedeker and earlier raids.

up my offer to visit the crash site. By then, I had established the identity of the two crewmen. They were Hptmn H Luttke (Staffelkapitan) and Utfz H Brillo. Smith's Sandpits is now an industrial estate, renamed Ford Road.

Colin Gray's list of battle credits includes:

August 31, 1940
9/JG26 Me Bf 109 E-4 (1184) shot down during escort sortie to Hornchurch. Forced landing on Jubilee Hall Farm, Ulcome, 6.45 pm. W Fronhofer captured, unhurt.

September 1, 1940
7/JG26 Me Bf 109 E-1 (3892). Engaged on escort sortie and engine damaged in combat. Forced landing at Newbridge, Iden, near Rye. J Burschgens captured unhurt.

People and planes dropping from the sky became an everyday event for East Anglians. Over Chelmsford, a rear-gunner from a crippled Heinkel bomber managed to jump to safety with his parachute only partly opened. Landing in a field near Althorne, he managed, despite injuries, to stagger to a cottage. The door was answered by Margaret Windridge who was rather disturbed to see a blood stained figure weakly waving a pistol. He meant no harm however – but simply wanted to surrender the weapon. Mrs Windridge dressed his wounds and treated him for shock until a military escort arrived to take the man prisoner.

Not all crashed airmen were so lucky – especially when rescuers weren't sure which side the victim was from ....

One British pilot shot down over East Anglia baled out and drifted towards a fruit farm. He was caught on one of the trees but was too badly burnt to free himself. Hanging there, he saw people approaching, and tried in vain to tell them through badly burnt lips that he was British. The farmer believing he had a Hun in his tree, jabbed the luckless flier with a pitchfork while his small son ran around the tree issuing threats in language quite unsuitable for a small boy. As the injured airman passed out, he remembers the mother telling the boy off for using bad language on a Sunday!

August 18 saw increased activity over East Anglia as the Luftwaffe concentrated on wearing down British defences with crippling day and night attacks. On one day alone, 398 HE bombs were dropped during daylight sorties, with 98 HE and over 300 incendiaries at night, killing 45 and injuring 200 across the region.

Wednesday, August 21
By day the enemy continued to fly in small raids of one or two aircraft, accompanied at times by another aircraft at a much greater height, the apparent object being to confuse the defences. His primary objective was aerodromes in the east and south east, and the secondary objective docks. It

is probable that the bombs dropped on the east coast were jettisoned by aircraft returning to their bases. By night, there was abnormally slight activity, probably due to adverse weather conditions.

Saturday, 31 August
By day, bombing was almost entirely confined to East Anglia, south and east London and Kent. In this area, three major raids developed: from 0755 to 0900 in East Anglia by 250 aircraft in five waves ....

.... In addition, single aircraft made reconnaissances of aerodromes in East Anglia during the morning, and in a small raid during the afternoon, reconnoitred the Thames estuary, Hornchurch and Kenley aerodromes, probably assessing damage previously caused. The apparent objectives in each case were aerodromes and communications. There was a considerable amount of indiscriminate bombing in East Anglia during the morning raid.

No. of bombs dropped: HE 107 plus, IB, 26 plus. Casualties (approx 19 killed, 78 seriously injured, 71 slightly injured.

By August 24, the Luftwaffe had changed its tactics. Instead of an all-out confrontation with mass raids across the North Sea, a new plan of night bombing raids aimed at industrial targets was introduced. It was left to Luftflotten 2 and 3 to weaken fighter command while Luftflotte 5 prepared to strike out against northern targets.

Damage to aerodromes, and loss of both planes and pilots put fighter command under severe pressure. By early September, Luftwaffe sorties increased with the launching of 1,000 daylight raids in an attempt to destroy strategic RAF bases.

From August 31 to September 6, Fighter Command lost 161 aircraft, the Luftwaffe 189. That week, 11 Group fought continuously to protect coastal targets and exposed airfields. That last day of August, a heavy force of enemy bombers strafed Cambridgeshire, Essex and Norfolk. The aerodrome at Debden was badly damaged by bombing. During the closing stages of this part of the Battle of Britain, dozens of young pilots paid the price of glory. Dorothy M Gregory, a nurse at Billericay Hospital remembers one of the casualties.

"I had been out for a cycle ride and was heading back towards the hospital when I stopped to watch two parachutes dropping to earth in flames. One of the parachutists, a young German was terribly burnt and died on a stretcher as he was being taken into the ward. I had to cut his clothing away and managed to rescue the eagle and swastika insignia from the tunic. The other airman, a British pilot, survived, although his life hung in the balance for several weeks. His wife refused to leave his bedside and tended him daily, changing his dressings and seeing to his needs."

For the Germans, there was no such event at the Battle of Britain. As far as the Luftwaffe was concerned, there was no break in the offensive; simply a change of tactics starting at the end of September with the escalation of night bombing raids against industrial targets.

After the fall of Dunkirk, extensive plans to launch 'Operation Sealion', the invasion of Britain, were discussed by German High Command. The Fuhrer was waiting impatiently for Goering to finish off the RAF before settling on an invasion date. On July 31, Hitler had a long conversation with Raeder, the naval C-in-C and accepted the view that 'Operation Sealion' could not be launched before the middle of September. There was some doubt whether the invasion could be attempted at all in that year if the Luftwaffe failed.

British invasion fears were reinforced by the arrest of four German agents picked up while landing from a rowing boat on the south east coast. The four men admitted they were spies, shipped in to report movements of British reserve formations in the Oxford/Ipswich/London/Reading areas during the weeks leading up to September 8 and 10, 1940.

From the end of the first week in September until mid-November, London and surrounding areas were blitzed nightly. German records report that 6500 tons of HE fell on chosen targets in October and nearly 2000 tons in November. East Anglia had special attention, especially the naval bases at Harwich, Yarmouth, Ipswich and Lowestoft. On the night of October 25, 16 bombers of the Italian airforce based in Belgium launched an attack against Harwich. One aircraft crashed on take-off; two got lost and no one seems to know for sure what happened to the rest. On the night of November 5, the Italians ventured across the Channel to attack Harwich with little success. They made a return trip on the 11th with a force of 10 bombers and 40 fighters for a daring daylight raid on Harwich. Three bombers and three fighters were shot down. A further ten fighters were damaged making forced landings. From October 25, 1940 to January 5, 1941, the Italians despatched some 87 bombers and 40 fighters against east coast targets, claiming to have dropped over 50 tons of bombs. Although several houses and industrial sites in Harwich, Lowestoft and Ipswich were strafed, causing structural damage and a handful of casualties, there were no fatalities.

The Germans decided that they would attempt to wear down the British will by making concentrated attacks against industrial sites and airfields. On the night of November 14/15, about 550 enemy bombers set out for Coventry. As they flew over East Anglia, they dropped a selection of parachute mines and bombs. They returned the next two nights to bomb south Cambridgeshire, Braintree and other smaller targets. On the 19th, a convoy was attacked between Yarmouth and Lowestoft. A crew member of HMT *Star of Pentland* was killed.

By now, the Germans had started using the X-Gerat direction finding system which greatly increased the accuracy of night bombing. Radar stations, searchlight and AA batteries had to be re-equipped to combat this, and training for night flying was increased. Among a series of mad schemes put forward to combat night attacks was the Admiralty plan to allow balloons carrying explosive charges to drift up towards incoming bombers. It was planned to launch a floating barrage 4000 feet high, seven miles wide and 55 miles long from strategic sites around the country. Over 900 mine carrying balloons were released on December 27 in the path of incoming bombers. Things went wrong from the beginning. About 300 of the balloons were ineffective and exploded pre-maturely, while others flew too high above the aircraft or crashed to earth.

Yet another aerial mine-field, known as LAM, the Long Aerial Mine, codenamed Mutton, was adopted by 12 Group and used over East Anglia in an attempt to reduce aerial activity. These mines were dropped by Havocs based at Coltishall and finally came into use in September 1941. Each aircraft carried 100 AD Type A Mk VII mines strung to a long

BEFORE, DURING AND AFTER THE RAID

HOT DRINKS IN THE SHELTER

—and the help that is ready if your home is hit

A hot drink is advisable before you go to sleep, particularly for the children. If you have not a thermos flask, you can make a " hay bottle " like the hay box used in cooking, which will keep a drink hot for hours.

HOW TO MAKE A "HAY BOTTLE"

Cut a square of any old woollen material, such as an old blanket, 8 inches longer than the length of the bottle. Line with either thin muslin or cotton material, sewing down the sides and leaving the top and bottom open, to be stuffed later on.

Cut two strips of the same woollen material, 8 inches to 10 inches long and 4 inches to 5 inches wide, rounded at one end. Line in the same way as the main square, for about two-thirds of the length, leaving a flap at the end. These are the side pieces. Mark the main square into three portions. Fold the lower portion over the centre portion making the lower half of a bag as in *Figure 1*.

Sew the two strips to each side of this case, thus filling in the sides of the bag as in figure 2. *Figure 2*

Stuff with straw, packed tightly, and sew down the lining.

Make a bag of American cloth similar to the woollen material one, but not lined or stuffed.

Place the bottle in the woollen bag, fold over and tuck in. Roll up and pin over.

Put this in the American cloth bag and roll up again. Tie a strip of material round it.

— After the Raid: —

IF YOU LOSE YOUR TOOLS OF TRADE

If your income is below a certain amount, you can apply to the Assistance Board for a grant to replace tools essential to your work, lost through air raids.

Help is ready if wanted

Injuries will be treated at First Aid Posts and Hospitals. If your house is damaged, you will get food, shelter, clothes and money if necessary. Try to arrange *now* with your friends to help them, but if you can't make such arrangements, you can go to the emergency Rest Centre if your house is bombed. The wardens and police know where it is. *Ask them.*

ISSUED BY THE MINISTRY OF HOME SECURITY

length of wire and suspended from a small parachute. The idea was that the falling web of explosives would be effective for about 20 minutes, by which time the invaders would fly right into the aerial barrage. Things certainly didn't go to plan. Several of the mines exploded prematurely, giving the enemy advance warning, while about 60 fell over Norwich, mining an area from the golf course to the heart of the city. Several houses were damaged, and an ARP warden, Herbert Batley died from wounds after triggering one of the devices.

Following the X-Gerat beam across East Anglia, a squadron of enemy bombers set out for Birmingham on the night of November 22/23. Flying high over the coast, they struck targets at Frinton, Colchester, Dunmow, Docking, St Neots and Cambridgeshire. Another hit and run raid on the 25th struck targets at Colchester, Frinton, Clacton and Bergholt.

Enemy activity was intense during the rest of the month. On the night of November 29/30th, 350 bombers strafed the region en-route to London.

In the three months from September, the number of raids on East Anglia were as follows:

	September	October	November
Essex	120	400	186
Suffolk	120	120	114
Norfolk	50	116	106
Cambs	31	95	49

Raids continued through December and into the New Year. The airfield at Stradishall was badly hit, with two dead and four injured. January saw renewed action against East Anglia.

January 4, 1941

Do 17Z of 11/KG3 observed dropping bombs at Valley Farm, Wherstead, Windows and roof extensively damaged.

0800 hrs, three armed reconnaissance flights observed. One entered over Southwold making for Coltishall and Norwich. The second flew in over Orford, touching Southwold. 10.00 hrs, Ju 88 machine-gunned Southwold.

January 7, 1941

Cambridgeshire attacked by Dornier 1/KG3. later in the day, 50 bombers carried out attacks against Norfolk, Suffolk and Essex. Airfields at Samford, Newmarket and Debden attacked. Bombs straddled offices at Honington. 15.35 hrs, Ipswich bombed and machine-gunned. UXB at Holywell Park. Later it was established to be a SD 1700 heavy fragmentation bomb which took the best part of a week to disarm and remove.

January 9, 1941

Flight of 300 enemy bombers observed over East Anglia. KG3 and KG53 dropped bombs over Clacton, Frinton (two parachute mines), Gorleston and Great Yarmouth.

January 15/16, 1941

Increased activity. 100 bombers flew in near Harwich. Dorniers of 11/KG2.

He 111's of KG4 carried out bombing raids against Samford, Felixstowe, Downham, Debden, Godmanchester, Smallborough and North Witchwood.

Early hours of l6th, a Ju 88 bombed Cambridge causing extensive damage to the Perse Boys School hall which was subsequently gutted by fire.

On January 29th, the weather was ideal for bombing and targets at Mildenhall, Norwich and Royston were machine-gunned.

The 30th saw more activity as bombers from KG2, KG4 and 11/KG2 brought havoc to the region. Parachute mines, HE, incendiaries and machine-gun fire kept the sirens active. A worker at the chicory factory in Lakenheath was killed. Two civilians died in an attack on Cambridge railway station.

Poor weather brought little respite. On February 1, 1941, Dorniers of 11/KG2 attacked Honington and Mildenhall, moving on to harass Yarmouth, Leiston and Little Fakenham. In Yarmouth, Grouts Silk Factory fell victim to several direct hits, resulting in two dead and ten injured. Leiston, Orford and Stowmarket were machine-gunned, causing extensive damage to property.

Activity increased with better weather. The night of February 17/18 was one of the worst on record for East Anglia. Norwich, Yarmouth, Attlebridge, Honington and Feltwell were all attacked. One of the worst places to suffer was Newmarket where over a dozen people died and many were injured when bombs reduced the main shopping area to rubble. Flying plate glass took a terrible toll.

As the days became lighter and brighter, hit and run raids gave way to night bombing sorties. Anti-shipping raids were increased, and on March 4, Dorniers of 11/KG3 attacked a convoy sailing off Cromer and Yarmouth. Shipping off Clacton was attacked on March 12. A new enemy tactic was to paint aircraft black, so that they could sneak in alongside returning British planes to shoot them up on landing.

Yarmouth was the victim on April 7. Incendiaries played havoc with communications. Severe damage was caused by two parachute mines which exploded over the north of the town. Fires swept through the area and soon became uncontrollable. Worse was to come. Soon after 5 am, two more parachute mines were dropped and fell into the inferno. One exploded at Middlegate Street, the other near Queen's Road. Five policemen were killed when their station collapsed around their ears. Seventeen people died and 68 were injured.

On April 9, two ships tied alongside Trinity Pier, Harwich, were blasted out of the water. The *Marnione* and the *Darcy Cooper* both received direct hits; the *Darcy Cooper's* crew of six were on board – and all were killed.

Bombs were also dropped on playing fields and the railway station. A searchlight and gun battery was peppered with machine-gun fire by low-flying aircraft. In Lowestoft, 300 incendiaries burnt down a cinema, a garage, several shops, the railway station and goods yard. Bombs continued to rain down on the blazing town throughout the night, destroying houses and cutting the railway line effectively disrupting communications.

By now, the enemy had learnt to fly under radar and dodge fighter patrols. Yarmouth, Lowestoft, Ipswich and several airfields were badly hit in the last two weeks of April. The Ferry Inn at Horning was destroyed in a particularly nasty attack on April 27/28 .

According to local rumour, the bomber pilot was attracted to the pub by headlights left on by a careless car owner. The bomb killed 22 people, including off-duty pilots from 222 Squadron. Visitors to the pub can see a plaque in remembrance of those who died in the raid.

Unbeknown to East Anglians, these attacks were to be the last of the major, concentrated sorties over the region until 1942. German bombers formerly stationed at Chateaudun, Schipol and Lille/Vendeville were off to Hitler's ultimate downfall.... the Russian Front.

On March 28, 1942, Bomber Harris despatched the first of his big raids to the Hanseatic port of Lubeck. A massive force of 234 bombers decimated the timber-built city. Hitler was furious and demanded a Terrorangriffe – a series of attacks likely to have the greatest possible effect on civilian life in Britain. Hitler chose his targets from the Baedeker guide book, selecting towns and cities of historical interest. Norwich was a prime target .....

At around 23.45 on April 27, a mixed force of Heinkels, Ju 88's and Dorniers dived towards the city. The railway station was the first to be struck, and being built mainly of timber, went up in flames, lighting the way for the rest of the bombers. Railway carriages, goods wagons, stores and workshops were engulfed by an inferno which spread to other parts of the city. To add to the chaos, the Germans dropped 250 and 500 kg high explosive bombs into the flames, and machine gunned streets at random. Water, gas and power mains were severed, hampering the work of the NFS.

ARP workers toiled until they dropped. Guides and Scouts acted as couriers, braving fire and bullets to carry messages. Former Patrol Leader Andrew Baker recalls that terrible night.

"There were about half a dozen of my troop posted to the Westwick Road CD depot and we had been given these big old cycles to deliver messages on. At first we managed OK, but soon we had to abandon the bikes because of punctures. The streets were full of broken glass and it cut the tyres to shreds. In the end, I found that by nipping up side streets and across back gardens, I could make better progress than by going across town. I don't recall being afraid, just excited as though on a rather realistic Scouting game. It was only after returning to our HQ and finding that it had been blown up that I suddenly realised it wasn't a game after all."

Food stores, pubs, clubs, a laundry and the Woodlands Hospital were destroyed during the 90-minute attack. Altogether, 20 factories were

The unexploded parachute mine that landed in Clacton was, at first, thought to be a hot water cylinder.

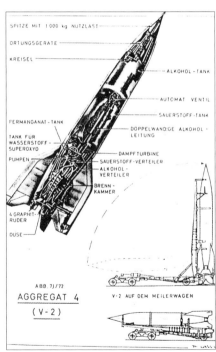

The V-2 rocket bomb brought a new wave of terror to Britain. Many either crossed or landed on East Anglia.

destroyed and 1250 people made homeless.

The last bomb was dropped at 1am, and within 30 minutes, a convoy of mobile canteens and field kitchens had moved in to cater for the victims and the emergency workers.

The Luftwaffe returned on April 29, when bombers of 11/KG2, 11/KG40. KG30 and IV/KG55 attacked Norwich and its surrounding area. The city was better defended this time as 252 heavy guns, Z rockets and light AA pieces had been moved into defensive positions.

Other raids followed, but on May 9, the Luftwaffe seemed intent on destroying what was left of the city. This time, the guns were ready for them. Gun batteries set up a concentrated barrage; Z rockets added to the confusion and balloons were hoisted to 3000ft to prevent low-flying aircraft attacking the target area. Light AA batteries on the outskirts of the city added to the flying hail of hot steel filling the night sky.

Several outlying towns and villages were strafed and bombed during this raid in which enemy bombers dropped 63 metric tonnes of bombs, including several parachute mines. Horsham St Faith, Stoke Holy Cross, Thorpe, Bramerton, Kirby and Caistor St Edmunds were all attacked.

The enemy didn't escape scot-free. A Do 217-4 snared the cable of a barrage balloon, and thrown off course and out of control, ran into a hail of AA fire, crashing close to Stoke Holy Cross.

From June onwards, things quietened down, restricted to tip-and-run raids, mine-laying and convoy hunting sorties. The Germans seemed to be playing a tit-for-tat game; lulling the defenders into a false sense of security, then attacking when least expected. This was the case on June 26/27, when Norwich was attacked. Just after 2 am, bombers from KGr.106, 7./KG100 and 111 KG2 roared in over the coast to drop around 10,000 incendiaries on the city, causing 650 fires. HE bombs added to the chaos. Norwich Prison, the tower of St Julian's Church, the railway telegraph office, a block of flats in Brook Place and the Corporation water tower were all hit. The cathedral was hit by incendiaries, but these were dealt with before they could do any damage. St Paul's and St Michael's were both devastated by fire. Nine people were killed and 22 injured.

On the 25th, bombers attacked Yarmouth, damaging 300 properties and killing three people. The town hall, police station and *Wrestler's Arms* pub were all hit.

Former fireman Ronald Bates remembers the Baedeker raids on the area as "a living nightmare".

"Originally, I had joined the AFS and was stationed on the outskirts of Caister, but with the introduction of the NFS, I found myself loaned out to other brigades in the area. Originally, I was posted to Yarmouth. Some of my mates had been drafted to Norwich during the bad raids over there, and told of terrible events. In one case, they found an entire family stone dead in their indoor shelter. The house had collapsed around their heads."

"When Yarmouth was bombed, everything seemed to go up in flames. We were swamped with calls and every one of us was out manning the pumps. It got so bad they had to call for outside help. Several of the HE's had ploughed up the road, damaging water and gas mains, so water pressure was low. It became so bad that some of our lads organised teams of ARP and CD workers armed with buckets of water and stirrup pumps to dampen down as best they could."

"One particularly bad job was a large furniture store crammed full of household effects. It blazed for hours. We managed to drag some of the stuff out but it had been terribly scorched and damaged by water from the hoses. Fumes from burning varnish and polish kept everyone back, and it was all we could do to stop the fire spreading."

"My job was branch-man, in charge of a hose. The one thing that sticks in my mind is the feeling of being so hot and wet. Being close to the flames, the front of me was scorching hot while my back was soaking wet as my mates played their hoses overhead with back-up jets. Being summer, it wasn't so bad, In winter, when the water almost froze as it came out of the hose, it was dreadful."

Later in the war, East Anglians were witness to Hitler's last desperate effort – the flying bomb.

During the 1930s, the Germans had devoted a lot of time and resources researching long-range rocket warfare. In December 1935, two liquid propelled rockets with gyroscopic stablisation were launched from the island of Borkum and reach a height of nearly one and a half miles. Throughout the early war years, dozens of rockets were launched with varying degrees of success, but none were capable of crossing the sea.

For almost a year before rocket attacks on Britain, RAF Photographic Reconnaissance and Central Interrogation Units had spotted strange looking buildings and ski-run structures while flying over the Peenemunde district. With the aid of partisan groups working under cover as labourers, the Allies had been able to obtain limited information on the German secret weapon. It was established that around 100 sites were near completion. If all of these were operational, 2000 missiles a day could fall on Britain.

The bomb being developed was the FZG.76, Vergeltungswaffe 1, or V-1. In Germany, it was known as the kirschkern (cherry stone) because of the sound of its engine. Here, blitzed Londoners called it the 'doodle-bug'. The bomb weighed about two tons, was 25ft long and had a 16ft wing span.

Despite rumours, the V-1 was not radio controlled, but was powered by a pulse-jet which worked for about an hour on low-grade aviation fuel. Its range was around 150 miles, later to be increased to 250 miles. Rockets launched from sites in Holland could, and did, hit London. A great many of these fell short in East Anglia.

The first four V-1s to be fired against England were launched on June 15, 1944. Within two days, over 100 had landed and the Home Secretary informed the House of Commons that the Germans had perfected the use of a pilotless plane.

Within the next few days, 100 rockets a day were droning in over the British coast. The rockets were released in salvos, and because they flew at high speed and low altitude, were difficult to shoot down. Eight single engine fighter squadrons, equipped with Spitfire IX, Tempest V, Spitfire XIV and Mosquito aircraft were used as flying bomb patrols. Mosquito XIXs were fitted with narrow-band centimetric radar, and in the right situation, could corner and disable the rockets. During July and August, 85 Squadron shot down 30 V-1s and 147 Squadron another 40.

For those who had survived the blitz, doodle-bugs were a worry. During the blitz, you could see – and hear – the enemy as he flew overhead. Doodle-bugs, with their nasty habit of suddenly cutting out and falling to the ground, were an unknown quantity. Although the numbers killed by these bombs was far less than during the blitz, their effect on people's nerves was severe. Whole families packed up and fled to the countryside. The Research and Experimental Department of the Ministry of Home Security was called in to study the trekking phenomenon, and concluded:

'The fact that many people chose to trudge off into the country each evening did not, by itself, imply a deterioration in morale. These people were afraid of bombs; of dark hours of wakefulness; of listening, sometimes tense and sometimes nodding, for the drawn-out whine, and the rumbling murmur of a house collapsing in the blackness. Above all, they wanted to sleep, for sleep was forgetfulness and rest. And to sleep - if only in a barn - was to behave normally; to lie awake was abnormal. So they dispersed themselves at night-time ...'

In Essex, Epping Forest played host to vast tented areas where the trekkers camped during the hours of darkness to escape the rockets.

East Anglians became used to seeing the rockets as they phut-phutted their way over the stretch of coast known as 'doodle-bug alley'. Mr H Burgess, who kept a wartime diary of air raids, recalls how he was nearly mown down by a flying bomb while keeping fire watch on the roof of an Eastern National bus garage. He had only just taken up his position by a tall chimney stack when he noticed a V-1 heading straight for him. "It was flying at about, 50-60 ft above the ground, and only just missed the top of the local cinema" he recalled. "It veered up Castle Road and headed straight for me." This particular doodle-bug landed in the grounds of Wivenhoe Park.

During September, Heinkel 111s began air-launching V-1s over East Anglia. One rocket nose-dived into a house just outside Ipswich airfield,

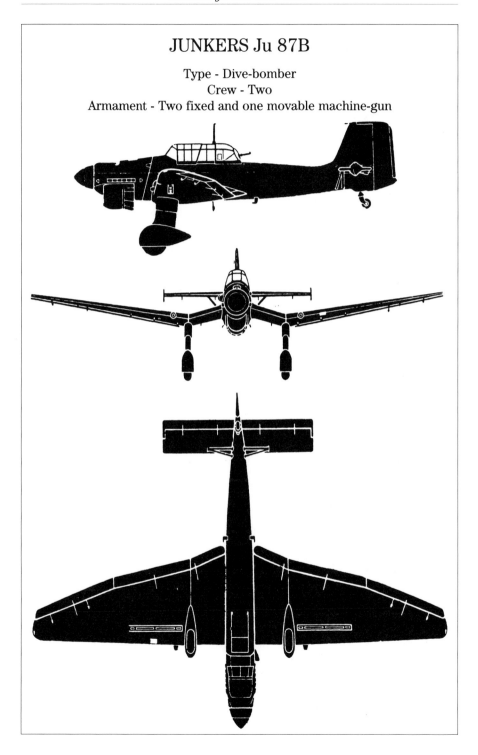

JUNKERS Ju 87B

Type - Dive-bomber
Crew - Two
Armament - Two fixed and one movable machine-gun

killing one serviceman and injuring others. On September 18, a rogue doodle-bug crashed on the airfield, causing several civilian casualties.

To combat the number of flying bombs being launched, a special Gun Belt known as a Diver Strip was introduced along the east coast. The aim was to blast the rockets out of the sky with a concentrated barrage of fire. The Home Guard manned Z rocket batteries in Norwich, Cambridge, Chelmsford and Colchester.

During June and July, Anti-Aircraft Command and Balloon Command under the leadership of Lieutenant-General Sir Frederick Pile and Air Vice Marshal W C C Gell were redeployed as a mobile defence against rockets. The idea was to shift the Diver Strip to whatever section of the coast was in line with flights of incoming rockets. It was aided by a web of high-flying barrage balloons and RAF fighters. The fighters attempted to gun the rockets down, or nudge them off course and back out to sea. Five fighter pilots died when they followed the rocket into the hail of fire from the Diver Strip.

During the summer of 1944, gun and balloon installations accounted for eight to ten rockets a day. Fighter squadrons despatched another 30, but even so, 50 a day were falling on Greater London and Essex.

The official log at Ford, Dagenham records:

PARTICULARS OF AIR RAID ALARMS ETC DUE TO FLYING BOMBS FROM 13TH JUNE TO 31ST AUGUST, 1944

	Hours	Minutes	
Time under public alert	635	12	
Time under danger signal	93	36	
Number of flying bombs plotted by Ford Motor Co			6869
Number of danger signals sounded in factory			791
Number of alerts sounded due to flying bombs			460

On September 8 the first long-range rocket fell on British soil at 6.40 pm. A few seconds later, another landed at Epping Forest. During the next two weeks, around 24 V-2's fell, many on Essex.

"I was working in a field near the marshes when I first saw these strange things rising in the air. They looked for all the world like stars going straight up into the sky until I lost sight of them" said Mr S Lummis, a farm worker at Beaumont, Essex, just after witnessing the launching of a V-2.

On September 25, a rocket attack was launched against Ipswich and Norwich. One missile fell at Hoxne, Suffolk. During the next three weeks, the enemy battery Lehr und Versuchs Batterie 444 launched 44 rockets against East Anglia; 32 crashed on land and five were seen falling into the sea. A number of near-misses were registered, with superficial damage in the Dereham Road and Mile Cross areas. Hellesdon golf course gained a new bunker when a V-2 exploded.

At first, the authorities kept news of the new rocket secret. The V-2 or A4 was a real rocket, something the Germans had been trying to perfect for years. The brainchild of Walter Dornberger and Dr Werner von Braun, it carried about nine tons of ethyl alcohol, water and liquid oxygen; was armed with a one ton warhead containing 1650 lbs of explosives and weighed about 13 tons. Its maximum range was 200 miles, rising to a height of 60 miles at peak trajectory. When striking a target, the missile tended to bury its nose in the ground, scattering debris over a wide area and making a crater about 4 ft by 27 ft in diameter.

A special radar with stations stretching from Lowestoft to Dover was introduced to pin-point rockets being launched from Europe. At one point, it was planned to increase the AA barrage along the coastal strip in a desperate attempt to blast rockets out of the sky as they passed overhead. The idea was shelved as there would have been damage to people and property from falling shrapnel.

During their short lifespan, 1115 V-2 rockets landed on Britian, with 400 of these falling on Essex.

Intensive search and destroy operations were launched by the RAF against V-2 sites. On February 14, 1945, Flt Lt Raymond Baxter, later to become famous as a television presenter, commanding A Flight 605 (City of Glasgow) Squadron stationed at Coltishall led a flight of Spitfire XVI's against a site in wooded dunes a few miles north of the Hague. After attacking the site several times, the airmen were some what taken aback to see, rising out of the woods in full

Issued by the Ministry of Health and the Department of Health for Scotland.

FIRST AID IN BRIEF

Read this carefully several times, then carry it in your pocket or bag

AFTER AN AIR ATTACK First Aid Parties will reach the wounded within a few minutes. Even such a short time counts. The man or woman on the spot can save lives by immediate and proper action.

Be prepared to see severe wounds. Be courageous and keep your head. Keep your mind on your duty to your injured fellow man.

Everyone in these days of danger should carry several clean handkerchiefs or small towels. These can be used as bandages, and their inner laundered surfaces are quite suitable for application to open wounds as a first dressing.

Unless a patient is in a highly dangerous place you should treat him where he lies. To lift or drag the wounded and transport should be left to trained parties. Your general rule is that the moving and transport should be left to trained parties.

The first and most important duty of the civilian helper who first reaches a casualty is to stop bleeding.

When you cut a thumb you naturally grab it firmly with the fingers of your other hand. That application of pressure to a bleeding wound is the correct thing to do in all cases.

TO STOP BLEEDING

Press on the bleeding point with fingers or hands. As soon as possible apply a clean thick pad of folded handkerchief or towel. Use an inner surface of your handkerchiefs or towels. Keep up the pressure through this pad. Bandage the pad firmly in position over the wound. Be sure that the dressing is applied firmly enough to control the loss of blood. If there is still oozing of blood past or through the pad renew pressure over the whole dressing.

BLEEDING FROM ARM OR LEG

Press on the wound with fingers or hands. Apply a clean thick pad as soon as possible. Keep up pressure through the pad. Bandage the pad firmly over the wound. If this fails, pass a bandage, tie, handkerchief, elastic or fabric belt, or similar article, round the limb as close to the wound as possible, at a point between the wound and the trunk. Knot the fabric so that the limb is loosely encircled. Pass a stick through the slack loop and twist till the tightening of the band round the limb stops the blood loss, taking care not to pinch the skin. Hold tight till the First Aid Party arrives. If you have to do this, make a note of the time when you tighten the loop and give it to the patient or attach it to the limb. It is very important that the hospital surgeon should know this.

majestic take-off, the gleaming body of a V-2. One pilot, Flt Sgt. 'Cupid' Love found he had the monster in line with his gun sights and blasted off a few rounds. As Raymond Baxter observed later: "Thank goodness he didn't hit anything vital or we wouldn't be here today to tell the tale."

The last rocket to reach Britain was observed by Ford spotters on March 27, 1945, and fell on Orpington. The last to be launched from a ground site against England was shot down at Orfordness in March 29 at 12.43 pm.

By the end of the war, around 5,000 tons of bombs had fallen on East Anglia. Unexploded bombs still appear today, and fishing boats still trawl up the odd mine or two off the coast. The wartime toll for Essex gives pause for thought .....

BOMBING OF ESSEX, 1939-45

13,972 high explosive bombs
1498 butterfly bombs
680 oil bombs
142,000 incendiaries
528 parachute mines (including 106 UXBs)
511 V-1s
400 V-2s

These caused 845 deaths and 5979 injured.

CHAPTER NINE

The Brylcreem Boys

Although air activity in the later part of the war was dominated by Americans, East Anglia was also home to many RAF bases. The 'Brylcreem Boys' as they were known by the less glamorous army, fought, and died, in the toughest early years of the war when Britain stood alone.

Fighter Command suffered its first casualty just three days after the outbreak of war. Pilot Officer Montagu Leslie Hilton-Harrop, aged 26, serving with B Flight of 56 Squadron was not killed by enemy action, but fell victim to the guns of fellow officers John Freeborn and Vincent Byrne, both of 74 Squadron.

At about 0615 on September 6, searchlight batteries reported to RAF Sector Operations in North Weald that a group of high flying aircraft had been spotted near West Mersea. It was assumed that these were enemy craft, sneaking in over the coast. Before anyone could establish otherwise, planes of 74 Squadron flew off, guns blazing. It was discovered too late that the 'enemy' was a flight of patrolling Hurricanes. Two aircraft were riddled with gunfire, resulting in the death of Hilton-Harrop who was shot in the back of the head. His plane crashed at Manor Farm, Hintlesham. His companion, Pilot Officer Frank Rose made a forced landing at Wherstead.

The affair caused something of a stir in RAF circles, but was classified Top Secret. The Station Commander, Section Controller, Byrne and Freeborn were all court martialled. Both pilots were acquitted. The event was to become known as the Battle of Barking Creek – why, no-one knows as Barking Creek is a good 50 miles from the actual site of the incident.

During the early hours of the morning on July 15, 1941, a light trainer aircraft flew low over the Essex coast and landed in a field close to Thorpe-le-Soken. On the face of it, this was nothing unusual. Country folk had become used to seeing planes landing in fields. This was no casual caller. The crew of two had escaped from occupied Belgium.

The men, Sgt Pilot Michel Donnet and Sgt Pilot Leon Divoy had both been in the Belgian Air Force. Donnet was taken prisoner in 1940, soon after

Belgian capitulation. He was repatriated in 1941 and immediately started to plan an escape to Britain where he could join the RAF and carry on the fight. All schemes seemed doomed to failure until he spotted a battered SV4B trainer unguarded in a shed a few miles from his home. Donnet realised that he needed a co-pilot to fly the relic and eventually established contact with Divoy, also keen to escape. Using odds and ends from an old alarm clock, they repaired the instrument panel. Fuel was a problem, but they managed to refine some high-octane from some black market fuel (the racket, it was later discovered, was run by a German serviceman). By July 4, all was ready, and donning their Belgian uniforms, they painted roundels on the wings of their liberated craft and took off for Britain.

After much coughing and spluttering, the engine finally caught and they roared off over the startled heads of a nearby German patrol. The patrol opened fire, but didn't do any significant damage. Harassed by flak and searchlights, they reached the North Sea. Forced by engine trouble to drop to 1000 feet, Donnet was relieved to see land. A second glance sent his heart plummeting into his flying boots for there on the roof of a building was the word 'Holland'. He couldn't believe his eyes – after all they had been through, they were going to land in enemy-held Holland! With just enough fuel left for about 20 minutes flying, he coasted down to find a landing strip. Making a successful touch-down near Daken's Farm, Frinton Road, Thorpe-le-Soken, Donnet and Divoy pushed the plane under a clump of trees and hid their firearms and maps in a clump of bushes.

The two airmen then set off down the lane, keeping an eye out for the Germans they believed were in occupation. Sergeant Percy Brown , the local policeman, had seen and heard the plane come down and, making his way to the spot, stumbled across the two men. Once at the police station, the two pilots managed to explain where they had come from. As all the evidence was hidden near the plane, it was decided to send Divoy, accompanied by Special Constable Charles Childs to recover the vital details and search the plane. By now the two had realised that they were in Britain, not Holland. If only they had seen the other part of the rooftop as they came in to land, they would have seen the word 'Motors'! The garage had once belonged to a flying enthusiast who had the name Holland Motors painted on the roof. It had been overlooked by the authorities.

Eventually, Donnet and Divoy were escorted to London and after interrogation, joined the RAF. Both were posted to 64 Fighter Squadron. Donnet ended the war as a Colonel with 375 combat missions to his credit, three enemy aircraft destroyed and six damaged. he holds the DFC, Croix de Guerre and four citations. Divoy crash landed over France in 1942 and spent the rest of the war in a POW camp.

Some years ago, Colonel Donnet returned to Thorpe in the hope of a reunion with his captors. Sergeant Brown had died the year before, leaving

Michel Donnet (astride aircraft) escaped from occupied Belgium in a stolen plane, landing at Thorpe-le-Soken on July 4, 1941.

Michel Donnet sitting in the rickety aircraft used for his daring escape to Britain, helped by fellow airman Leon Divoy.

78-year-old Charles Childs the sole surviving witness of the landing.

At the end of the war, the old Stampe Vertongen 4B trainer was ferried back to Belgium where it can be seen on display in the Musee de l'Armee in Brussels.

By early spring of 1942, plans were being formulated by Sir Arthur 'Bomber' Harris and Frederick Lindemann for the blanket bombing of Germany. After the initial raid on Lubeck – which brought Hitler's Baedeker reprisals – he assembled the first 1000 bomber attack on Cologne. Sgt Flight Engineer Harold W Curtis took part in this attack with 78 Squadron. Returning from the raid, his Halifax Mark I bomber was involved in a mid-air collision with a Hampden bomber over March. As both aircraft fell to the ground in flames, Curtis managed to parachute to safety. Landing heavily, he wrenched his left leg but managed to hobble over to the wreckage and help the Home Guard to remove the dead and injured. One over-zealous Home Guard, spotting a parachute flare among the debris evacuated the entire area, leaving the lame sergeant stranded in the middle of the field. The poor fellow had to limp a mile and a half to the main road before being picked up by the local doctor.

Out on Sudbourne Marsh, between Aldeburgh Bay and Orford, there was a live ammunition battle zone. The idea was to create a realistic backdrop for the troops prior to setting out for the real thing. Squads of men were drafted into the area, entrenched in fox-holes and systematically bombarded by missiles, usually pitched to fall short or pass overhead. One night, a British destroyer lying close to shore, lobbed shells into Orford instead of the battle zone. Fortunately, no one was killed or injured.

There were, of course, many accidents in and around the live ammunition zone. One fatal incident concerned Group Captain H W G Penderel, one of the greatest characters in the RAF who was killed over Sudbourne Marshes on May 14, 1943 while conducting secret bombing raids.

Hubert Wilson Godfrey Jones (he adopted the name Penderel by deed poll in the late 1920's) joined the 4th Btn Welsh Rgt T F on the outbreak of the Great War. Godfrey (he didn't like being called Hubert) was a great adventurer and found life in the trenches rather slow so volunteered for the more exciting RFC. He had a natural aptitude for the job, and in 1917 won the Military Cross.

During the post war years, he served as Squadron Leader of No. 19 Flight, 216 Squadron at Heliopolis. Always something of an eccentric, he earned himself the nickname 'Bats' due to his unorthodox flying methods.

Unorthodox or not, he won the King's Cup Air Race in 1927.

During the 1930s, Penderel discovered a little known track through the Quatora Depression which became listed on wartime maps as Penderel's Track. It was used extensively by Colonel Stirling's Long Range Desert Group in the behind-the-line raids of 1942. In 1931 Penderel led a flight of

Group Captain Colin F Grey shot down the Me which landed in Smith's sandpits, Clacton. Inset: *The irrepressible 'Bats' Penderel.*

three Victorias to Cape Town and back, and was awarded the Air Force Cross in June of that year.

Brigadier Harold Kirby, writing from South Africa, recalls the time Bats was stationed with his group during the desert campaign.

'He used to fly his Gladiator in the desert with a large chameleon tied to the gunsight with a piece of cotton to keep the flies away. He completely ignored windsocks, and landed in a straight line along the direction of his arrival at the airfield. He once took an unsuspecting army type up in a Hawker Hart one day, and swung on landing, ending up with the nose in the deck and the tail in the sky. The army type thought that was quite normal, we were all convulsed with laughter.'

At the time of his death, Penderel was attached to the Station Flight of RAF Middle Wallop, flying Hurricane HV895. He soon became involved with secret bombing trials over East Anglia, and although 52, handled his plane with the speed and skill of a youngster. On the day of his death, an eye-witness observed him taking off with what appeared to be two large 40 gallon drums slung under the wings of his Hurricane.

Brigadier Kirby concludes: "From what I can remember of the death of 'Bats', as recounted in the newspaper and also from stories circulating in our Group of the Desert Airforce, he was experimenting with some sort of napalm or similar weapon. He was doing low level bombing, and the weapon ricocheted off the ground and struck his Hurricane, setting the fabric-covered elevators alight. Whether he was aware of the damage or not, he had no control of the looping plane and crashed."

Penderel's stricken plane crashed close to Red House Farm, Sudbourne on May 14, 1943. His body was cremated at Ipswich on May 17.

East Anglian author Gordon Kinsey, delivering one of many interesting talks on aviation during the 1970s recalls how, at the end, an old lady approached him and introduced herself as a relative of the late Group Captain Penderel. She told him how upset the family had been to hear of Godfrey's death – not so much because of the way he had died, but because his ashes were never brought home to Wales. "Lost en-route" was the far from satisfactory official explanation.

Research has revealed very little of an official nature, but interviews with former personnel who served on these secret bases reveals that experiments were carried out, not only with napalm, but also with nerve gases and a special anthrax bomb much favoured by Churchill. Fortunately, this bomb was never officially used.

CHAPTER TEN

The Yanks are Coming

Although America did not officially enter the war until the Japanese attack on Pearl Harbour on December 7, 1941 (two years late according to some), the USA had been pursuing a covert policy of economic warfare against the Axis powers since 1939. Although officially neutral, the Americans had been supplying arms and equipment to the British long before official involvement in the war.

Aircraft manufactured in the USA were transported to the Canadian border, where they were 'borrowed', then flown across the Atlantic to become part of the British war machine. American pilots, hungry for action, often volunteered to fly the aircraft so that they could get to Britain and join in the fight.

East Anglia played host to our American allies for the duration of the war. Norwich, ringed by Liberator bases had more than its fair share of Americans, wryly described as "over-paid, over-sexed and over here". Nearly 100,000 acres of Norfolk farmland were taken over by the USAAF, and by October 1942, the sound of aircraft engines from fields such as Debden, Horham, Aldermaston, Wattisham, Duxford, Goxhill, Horsham St Faith, Aycham, Bassingbourne, Tibenham, Bodney and North Pickenham could be heard night and day. Airfields were usually built by the British, with American engineer battalions assisting with their more sophisticated equipment. A typical airfield occupied 500 acres and had three concrete runways, the main runway normally 2000 yards long. Each base was equipped with two independent fuel points.

The locals either loved or hated these exotic new arrivals. Glamorous, gum-chewing, apparently rich and far more sophisticated than the local boys, they were universally popular with the female population. Gifts of sweets, tinned foods, nylons and silk underwear, all delivered with a liberal helping of transatlantic charm were irresistible to the girls. The local lads, permanently broke, wearing shabby wartime clothes and without transport hadn't a chance against these New World newcomers.

Once the Yanks had settled down and made friends it became obvious that much of the brashness was a cover for shyness – and they weren't too sophisticated not to fall for a good old English leg-pull. One of the best concerns Soane's memorial to Michael and Philippus Hills in Colne Park. American servicemen in the area were driving the locals wild with stories about the good old USA – and were drinking all the beer. One evening in the pub one of them asked what was in the urn on top of the Hills' memorial. "Thass fulla liquid gold" one local assured him, tongue in cheek. Nothing else was said, but a couple of nights later, the muffled sound of machine-gun fire was heard in the village. Later, it was discovered that the urn was riddled with bullet holes, still visible today.

The most striking thing about these Americans was their extreme youth. Most were aged between 17 and 21. One group, 'The Bloody Hundredth' returning to base after suffering horrific losses found that the oldest gunner left was just 17. He returned to an empty billet. All his comrades had been lost in action.

In three years, the 8th Air Force suffered 6456 casualties, lost 5600 aircraft, flew 330,523 sorties and dropped 732,321 bombs. The 8th despatched 6230 enemy aircraft in the air and 3079 on the ground. A visit to the American war cemetery at Maddingley just outside Cambridge bears testimony to the tremendous price they paid.

USAAF activities around East Anglia caused more actual damage than the enemy. Aircraft making faulty take-offs had a nasty habit of jettisoning bombs over the nearest field. Bury St Edmunds had a near miss when an American bomber ditched its load nearby. There was another near miss for nearby villages when the bomb supply blew up at Metfield. A drone packed solid with explosives crashed into a wood at Sudbourne Park, Suffolk clearing the timber up to 200 yards away. People around Harrington didn't like the look of matt black aircraft seen leaving the field. This sinister disguise was vital – the planes were headed for enemy territory, laden with arms containers, leaflets, pigeon hampers and new agents for the Resistance and Secret Army.

Local feeling didn't bother the Americans too much. What they hated was the lack of home comforts. Used to electricity, hot water, mountains of food and drink and ever-open bars, the restrictions and shortages of rural wartime England were a horrible shock. The natives didn't seem too friendly either ... American pilots were apt to forget the recognition signal when returning from raids and were furious when AA batteries opened fire as they slipped in over the coast. Gunners could be trigger-happy and slipshod on aircraft recognition. As late as 1944, a RAF Beaufighter was shot down over Colchester by a Liberator's excited tail-gunner.

American airmen were undoubtedly brave – sometimes to the point of being foolhardy. Who but an American would smuggle the exiled Prince

A P-38 Lightning ready for action.

Members of the 479th Fighter Group, Wattisham. F/O Raymond King (second left, front row) died from exposure when his plane Little Ziggy ditched off Holland-on-Sea.

Bernhard of the Netherlands aboard a bomber of the 489th and take him for an illicit joy ride over enemy territory!

Another incident involving US servicemen had more serious consequences. It was December 3, 1944 and Sir Eric Teichman, distinguished traveller, diplomat and expert on Chinese affairs had just finished lunch at his home, Honingham Hall near Norwich. Hearing the sound of gunfire from his woods, Sir Eric went to investigate and stumbled across a pair of GI's armed with carbines. He challenged them and was promptly shot dead.

As a result of joint investigations carried out by the USAAF and Norfolk police, two men were arrested. One of them, George E Smith Jnr of Pittsburgh was charged with murder. At his court martial held at Attlebridge on January 9, 10, 11 and 12, Smith, aged 27, was shown to have been a constant source of trouble. He had already appeared before a court martial on eight previous occasions. On the day of the murder, Smith in company with Private Leonard S Wojtacha had been drinking. The pair broke into the camp armoury, stole the carbines and ammunition and decided to go poaching in the grounds of Honingham Hall. Smith pleaded not guilty on grounds of insanity, and was cool to the point of being cocky throughout the trial. He was sentenced to death on January 12, 1945.

Another strange yarn concerning American fliers was told to me by an ex-USAAF Colonel back in the 70s. The story concerned a group of fliers based at Rougham. Being of German extraction, these men refused point-blank to strike at German targets because they might be dropping bombs on relatives. The men were grounded until replacement crews arrived from the States, but a number of planes were sabotaged. When the bombers finally set off on a mission, several were supposed to have blown up over the Channel. A secret investigation was carried out, several arrests were made, and after a drum-head court martial, a number of men were executed on the spot. Older locals will tell you that the bodies are buried in Rougham Churchyard. Investigation of church records and USAAF files reveals nothing – but both American and British officials are past masters at 'losing' embarrassing skeletons from the past.

Then there was the 861st Engineer Aviation Battalion and the curse of the witches' stone. These stones, standing about three feet high and measuring around 80 inches at the base can be found in Essex, Suffolk, Norfolk, Buckinghamshire, Oxfordshire and beyond. They are thought to date back to 5000BC and may have been used as milestones by nomadic tribes – or as altars in Black Magic ritual. A long standing legend warns dire consequences to anyone removing or damaging one of the stones.

Intent on building a base at Borham, the engineers of the 861st found a witches' stone in the path of a road-widening scheme. The locals refused point blank to move it so the CO called in a bulldozer which was badly damaged trying to move the stone. Things went wrong from then on. The bulldozer driver was killed when a bomber overshot the runway and landed on the bulldozer, killing both the driver and the aircrew. The CO, Lt Col Stanley H Lomax was struck down by a heart attack on June 5, 1944. The stone can still be seen in the car park of the *St Anne's Castle* pub, Borham.

The Americans took part in many of the mass bombing campaigns of the war, and in secret operations against V1 rockets. One afternoon in August 1944, a Boeing B17 Flying Fortress was seen over the villages of Chillesford and Tunstall. At first, villagers ignored it – planes were a common sight – but then a solitary parachutist was seen. Almost immediately, the bomber banked steeply in a downward dive and exploded in Watling Wood near Sudbourne Park. The lone survivor, Master Sgt Elmer Most, aged 24, claimed to be one of a nine-man crew returning from a bombing mission over Europe. The pilot, Lt John Fisher Jnr perished in the explosion. Sworn to secrecy about the true nature of his flight, Sgt Most convinced the British authorities into believing his story. In reality, the aircraft was a secret guided missile used by the Americans in their anti V-I campaign.

On August 12, two more Americans prepared to fly their PB4Y Liberator against a target in Heligoland. They were Lt Joseph P Kennedy (elder brother of Jack, Bobby and Teddy), and Lt Wilford J Willis, both members of the USNR. Once airborne, the two men took their 21,170 lb flying-bomb to 15,000 feet and prepared to jump out over the Blyth estuary. They threw the switch to arm the missile, and knew no more as the plane was destroyed by two almighty blasts. Damage was spread over a six-mile area. A few years ago, one of the East Anglian Aircraft Research Units managed to locate the engines, part of the undercarriage and the bomb doors and returned some of the remains to the American authorities for metallurgical tests.

The brave young men who volunteered for this hazardous job had no doubt that their work was dangerous. The chances of things going wrong were very high. War historians on both sides of the Atlantic have wondered why Joseph Kennedy, a young man whose future was assured, should have volunteered to chase adventure in a stripped-down war-weary bomber loaded with explosives.

The idea of launching unmanned drone aircraft against strategic enemy positions had been devised in direct response to the threat from rockets. The first NOBALL (code name for enemy launching sites) missions had taken place during Christmas 1943 when several flights of B17 bombers and B24's had unsuccessfully bombed experimental rocket workshops and launch sites. Frustrated by the failure of normal bombing, the USAAF authorities thought up Project Aphrodite. The job of stripping out bombers, fitting them with radio controlled equipment and filling them with explosives fell to the 562nd Group stationed at Fersfield, Norfolk.

In theory, the plan was simple.The Aphrodite drone was to be launched manually by volunteer pilots such as Kennedy and his companion. Once the bomb was working well, the pilots were to throw the fuse control switch and parachute to safety over the coastline. A control aircraft flying alongside would then guide the primed bomber to its target.

To all intents and purposes, the explosion killed Kennedy. But, did it? In 1986, a startling story hit the headlines. A former Luftwaffe artillery officer claimed to have captured Joseph Kennedy on French soil on July 14, 1944, a month before he was reported killed in the drone explosion. Karl-Heinz Wehn, a 23 year old lieutenant of the Luftwaffe Flakkorps was serving with the 1st Regiment, 13th Battery, south west of Caen when a flight of American four-engined bombers came into view. Flying at over 4300 metres, they were well out of range of AA guns and flew unchallenged over Caen and Lisieux making for Soissons. The aircraft were heading for a secret rocket site. It had also been revealed by the Resistance that Hitler had visited one of these bunkers on June 17, and was believed to have remained in the area, keeping an eye on progress.

Wehn was part of a gun battery dug into the side of a low hill near St Andre, an ideal observation point. As the flight of bombers continued unhindered towards their target, Wehn's attention was turned to a more immediate threat from Lightning fighter bombers attacking the 12th Panzer Division grouped near the River Orne. The gun batteries took on the fighters in a fierce battle and it was another hour before Wehn heard more of the bomber flight, now reported to be heading back to base. This time, the bombers were lower, an ideal target for Wehn and his gunners.

"The bombers split up and peeled off in all directions, diving to the left and right, " recalls Herr Wehn. "It was certainly no use firing haphazardly at the whole group so we concentrated on just one aircraft. I fired ten salvos of four shots each at the bomber which was, by now, right in the eyepiece of my range finder. As I gave the order to fire, the plane seemed to bank in a left-hand curve, making towards the English Channel and exposing its entire flank to our battery. We couldn't miss and a number of shots struck the fuselage near the rudder section. The aircraft caught fire and started to fall. Just before the first burst of flame, we saw two parachutes – too soon I thought. If they had waited until the plane was lower, they would have landed in British-held territory."

"The plane crashed into the sea at Bayeux and the two parachutists came down in a field about 1km from our gun position, out towards Grimbosq. They ran into a wood. About ten minutes later, two soldiers from the 12th Panzer Division approached the wood, calling out to the men to give themselves up. Realising there was nowhere to go, the two Americans came out of the wood and surrendered. They gave no trouble."

"A little while later, I made my way to the bunker where the prisoners were being kept to interrogate them. The British troops on the other side of

GI ground crew checking machine-gun cartridge belts for faulty linkage – which could be fatal in action.

Left: *A GI engineer poses on a section of metal runway.*
Right: *Sgt Lou Biernat checking the 'teeth' of one of his charges before take-off, 1944.*

the river could see all this quite clearly, but didn't attempt to fire at us. The rules on POWs meant that the Americans could only be processed by ground troops in charge of that area. As I was a Luftwaffe officer, I had no say. I explained this to the two men and invited them into the bunker. I told them to await transport to a camp, but said it might take some time. One of the Panzers tried to establish contact with his HQ. He finally got through, and my orders were to keep the men safe until an escort party could be sent to escort them to a camp. The taller of the two men said 'that's just my bad luck. I could have gone home today. How long do you think I will be in prison.' I told him about a year."

Karl-Heinz Wehn captured a man calling himself Joe Kennedy.

Wehn then interrogated the men. The interview took about 40 minutes, and was the usual set of questions on name, weapons, home base, target, wounded in the damaged aircraft etc.

The second prisoner wasn't questioned. only asked his name which he said was Master Sergeant O' Patrick.

The first prisoner said his name was Joe Kennedy, First Lieutenant, US Air Force. "I didn't understand at first," Wehn recalls, "and asked him to repeat this. He did, adding that he was from Hyannisport, near Boston, Massachusetts, USA. When I asked him what he did before the war, he said he helped his father. When I asked him what his father did, he said he was the American Ambassador in London before the war, then owned a shipping company in Boston."

During the routine search of the prisoner's effects, Wehn found a small identity plate, 6 cm long and 0.5 mm thick, fastened to the chest pocket of his coverall. It was stamped with his name and rank, exactly as detailed in the interrogation.

"Later that evening, the two prisoners were handed over to a detachment of SS and that was the last time I saw them alive," says Wehn. "About 21.15, I heard a commotion coming from the direction of the river bank, followed by gunfire. A general alarm was raised and I was given to understand that members of the SS camped by the river had seen two men in flying kit

Joe Kennedy, brother of Jack, Bobby and Teddy was apparently killed when his Liberator exploded over the Blyth - but a German witness reported him captured and shot a month earlier.

running towards the water. The men jumped into the river as the SS opened fire. Five minutes later, medical orderlies pulled Kennedy and the other man out of the water. Both were dead. The bodies were buried on 15 July, 1944 just outside the little churchyard of St Andre sur Orne. The marker says 'two unknown foreign soldiers."

The German officer responsible for the death report was SS Kapitan Eric Olboeter, but his files and reports were destroyed in the bitter fighting around Falaise Gap. Olboeter was badly injured in the battle and died on his way to hospital.

The official account of young Kennedy's death has been the subject of several books and magazine articles. In *The Kennedys - an American Drama*, we learn how Joe Junior practised flying the stripped-out bomber, loaded with ten tons of sand to simulate the load it would eventually carry.

'On August 11, the night before take-off, in the plane called *Zootsuit Black*, Kennedy stalked around the barracks, nervous and annoyed because he was not allowed to bicycle to a call box to make a goodbye call to Pat Wilson. He said he was sorry he had even volunteered for the job, but when electronics officer Earl Olsen took him aside to say he was uncertain about the circuits and wanted time to make some changes, Joe wasn't in the mood to listen. " I appreciate what you are trying to do, but I don't have any say about things like that. I just volunteered to fly" he told Olsen. Olsen pressed him to ask for a delay until the electrical system was changed. Kennedy repeated that he had already volunteered. "Sure you volunteered" Olsen said, " and you can un-volunteer too, don't you see? You're risking your neck for nothing." Olsen pleaded with him to see the commanding officer about putting the mission off. "No," Kennedy said finally. "I don't think I will, I'm going to fly."

Olsen's warning was, in fact, warranted as it was thought that a short-circuit had caused the plane to explode when the arming switch was thrown.

As Kennedy climbed into *Zootsuit Black*, another pilot asked him if his insurance was up to date. Giving that famous grin, Kennedy said "nobody in my family needs insurance". He took off in the early evening. Twenty eight minutes after take-off, the code words 'Spade Flush' were given - followed immediately by an enormous explosion. The concussion damaged support aircraft, causing them to make an emergency landing. A reconnaissance aircraft flying with the mission carried Joe's close friend Elliott Roosevelt, son of the President, who witnessed the disaster first hand.

So who was the American flyer calling himself Joe Kennedy, captured and later shot by German forces in France a month before the official loss of *Zootsuit Black*? Was it perhaps another Joseph Kennedy? Someone who realised that the son of a prominent American might have an easier time as a prisoner than an ordinary airman? If this was the case, why the escape attempt? We will never know.

Literally hundreds of young Americans died on missions flown from East Anglian bases, some in mid-air collisions, some in combat, some returning to base. Such was the case of Raymond King, a 22-year-old flying a P-51D Mustang, *Little Zippie*. Returning from a combat mission over Worms on January 13, 1945, the Mustang developed engine trouble and King was forced to ditch about a mile from the coast. He managed to escape from the cockpit, and although rescued by lifeboat 20 minutes later, died in hospital from exposure. The wreckage of the Mustang was to stay on the sea bed until 1987. It was the bane of local fishermen as it constantly snagged trawl nets and equipment. In 1987, members of the East Essex Aviation Museum decided to try and salvage the Mustang. After several survey dives, the remains were found and recovered. The plane was remarkably well-preserved. The instrument panel – still intact – showed the clock stopped at 3.40 soon after the aircraft hit the water. Museum members cleaned and restored the Mustang and managed to contact members of Raymond King's family who kindly gave letters, documents and his certificate for the Purple Heart for display with the plane. The East Essex Aviation Museum is at Point Clear, Essex.

American wartime memorabilia is in short supply in this country, but one recent acquisition is the wartime diary of Carroll C Sprague, Base Photo Lab, 479 Fighter Group, Wattisham, Suffolk, an intriguing photographic and written record of the war years. On the inside cover, he describes his journey from the USA.

ENGLAND 1944 - 45

'I sailed from New York on May 2, 1944 and after an eventful fourteeen days – during which time one destroyer in our convoy managed to sink a German submarine, saving the ship I was on, the *Argentina*, a 50,000 ton passenger ship converted for troop carrying purposes. On that one ship there were about eight thousand men and two hundred and fifty WACs. The *Argentina* was the flagship of the convoy and well protected on all sides. A daily routine on shipboard was to have an abandon ship drill at about 10 am and again in the afternoon at 2.30. As before mentioned, it took fourteen days to cross the Atlantic and pass the Azores ... then up to the northern part of Ireland, finally landing at Gourock, Scotland. We put into harbour at about 2 am on the morning of May 16 and from then until about 11 am, we stayed on the ship waiting for the ferry taking us to shore, then marching on to the train which was right there waiting for us. There the British Red Cross served us coffee and donuts which tasted good after the poor food on board the ship.

We left Gourock about 2 pm that day for an eighteen-hour trip taking us through Edinburgh, where we saw our first castle. The English trains are of narrow gauge and the carriages are divided into eight compartments. Each compartment is large enough for eight people on two seats facing each other. We finally arrived at Stowmarket in Suffolk County where we were to get off. At about ten in the morning on May 17, we were loaded on to army trucks which took us to the place which was to be our home base for the next seventeen months. The station was named Wattisham.'

'The first question we asked was "where's the mess hall" and the second question "where do we sleep". After eating, we went to our barracks and most of us took showers, made up our beds and got things ready for living as comfortably as possible – then some of us started an exploration of the base and came to the American Red Cross building and HQ and got a look at the rest. Many found the *Little Wheels* club and got their first taste of English beer .... most of them said it tasted like P.... A few of my friends and myself preferred to walk around and see what the place was like. We went out to the runway and looked back towards the base .....'

Carroll C Sprague survived the war but was killed in a flying accident in 1946.

CHAPTER ELEVEN
The Road to Victory

*B*y the beginning of 1944, the war in Europe was beginning to swing in favour of the Allies. The Red Army was advancing in the east, the British and Americans were preparing 'Operation Overlord' in the west, and victory was in the air. Despite strenuous German attempts to discover the invasion plan, D-Day remained top secret. Hitler believed invasion would come in Normandy, but his High Command favoured Calais. As it turned out, Hitler was right, but lacked evidence to support his theory.

The Luftwaffe continued bombing and strafing raids against strategic targets, but raids were few and far between now, with just a dozen German aircraft making daylight attacks on Britain during the latter part of 1943.

December saw increased activity, with a raid against Gosfield aerodrome on the night of the 10 th. About a dozen Do 217s blitzed the area with an assortment of missiles, but caused little damage, Earl's Colne and Wethersfield were attacked on the same night. Several enemy fighters were destroyed by British night fighters patrolling the coast.

January 1944 started quietly, but on the evening of the 21st, air raid sirens warned of over 100 German aircraft intent on a Baby Blitz against London. Approaching East Anglia, several bombers dropped a scattering of explosives over March, Braintree and Newmarket.

This attack was code-named 'Operation Steinbock' and commanded by General-Major Dietrich Pelz with the aim of crippling docks, factories and invasion force bases. In East Anglia, special attention was paid to the phantom invasion force, FUSAG, thought by the Germans to be sheltering around Woodbridge and Rendlesham Forest. This was, in reality, a huge decoy site which succeeded in bluffing the enemy.

Well over 600 night attacks were made against East Anglia during January, with the loss of 36 enemy aircraft. A concentrated barrage of AA, searchlights and balloons made life difficult for the Germans.

February, March and April saw the swan song of Operation Steinbock. Throughout this period, the enemy attacked night and day, with targets stretching from Southend to Southwold. April 18/19 saw widespread bombing of the region. Targets included Stonham, Sheringham, Westleton and Little Snoring. Several British planes returning from missions over Europe fell foul of German aircraft. By now, the Luftwaffe was attempting to play the RAF at its own game, lurking around airfields to attack returning flights as they landed.

As the war progressed into its final phase, the first batches of German prisoners arrived in East Anglia. Italians from North Africa were first, followed by the Germans. In brown or green battledress, marked with a large circle or diamond in contrasting colour, the men worked on the land, airfields and bomb-damaged buildings. Much to the surprise of the locals, these men turned out to be quite human!

POW camps were erected all over the region, and after work, the prisoners sat in Nissen huts around a hissing Tilley lamp carving wonderful examples of treenware. In pre-war days, many of the Austrian prisoners had been clock makers. They made peacocks, families of pecking chickens, hobby horses and many other toys, all gratefully received by toy-starved British children. Toys were made from scrap wood, carved with a piece of glass or a fragment of razor. Although fraternisation was strictly forbidden, these beautifully made toys sold as quickly as they were made. Cigarettes were favoured currency among the POW's. Examples of POW treenware do turn up from time to time in local antique shops and at auctions. Most have survived the test of time.

The prisoners also produced concerts to entertain themselves and local villagers. Costumes and props were made from whatever was available. Make-up was soot scraped from Tilley lamp glass, boot polish or walnut stain.

Towards the end of the war, these men were almost free, and allowed to run their own lives and camps in some areas. Once hostilities had ended, they were used to clear land-mines from cliff tops and beaches. Repatriation was a problem. Many came from towns and villages now occupied by the feared Red Army, and decided to stay in Britain or emigrate to Canada, Australia or New Zealand rather than return home to an uncertain future under Communist rule.

Although one hears very little of escape attempts, a party of Luftwaffe pilots tried to steal an aircraft from a field near their camp. Stationed at 186 POW camp, Colchester, former prison guard 4808471/Lc/Bm A Jones, RA, remembers the night when seven Luftwaffe officers escaped from the compound. The area was cordoned off and roads, houses and barns searched. They were eventually captured at Boxted aerodrome where they had managed to slip past patrolling sentries to try and start a number of fighters. Failing to work the auxiliary engine, they set about sabotaging the planes by pouring sand and gravel into fuel tanks.

German POW concert party at Beaumont, Essex.

A victory poster, issued in 1945, could be seen in most homes.

Coastal regions were, of course, in the thick of the action once invasion plans were under way – as wartime diarist Mr A B Kennell of Holland-on-Sea reports:

January 5th, 1944
All empty houses in Holland-on-Sea occupied by troops. Lorries and guns line all the roads.

7th
Saw 269 Yank planes in one bunch this morning, followed by another 100, then still more. Got fed up counting.

February 14th
Last night's raid was the worst we have had for a long time. Flares hung over the town and crowds of incendiary bombs fell all over the place. The electricity was cut off ..... Marks and Spencers, Fairbains, Boots and Catlins burnt out. The Odeon was hit and two hotels. We shot down six planes. Have been working on bomb damage repairs all day.

23rd
In last night's raid over Clacton, incendiary bombs destroyed several houses, including Dr Moore's which was burnt out. 60,000 incendiary bombs have been dropped in this area during the last ten days.

March 21st
A ten mile travel ban is being put on a strip of coastline stretching from the Wash to Land's End, starting 1st April.

April 3rd
All the guns fired on Holland cliffs today, including 6 in naval, 4.5 and 3.7 AA guns, Bofors and machine-guns. It was like bedlam.

21st
Last night kept awake until early dawn by a great force of 1150 4-engined bombers. They dropped 4000 tons of bombs over occupied Europe.

May 1st
This morning at 5.30 am awakened by planes flying low overhead, dropping flares and signalling to each other. Is it a practice test for the invasion?

May 3rd
All leave has been stopped for the army, navy and RAF. Is it the 2nd Front ?

'VE' Day, Victory in Europe, was officially announced in East Anglian newspapers on Tuesday May 8, 1945, although the actual ceremony of surrender had taken place on May 7 at 2.41 am, French time. Newspapers such as the East Essex Gazette brought out special rush editions announcing the

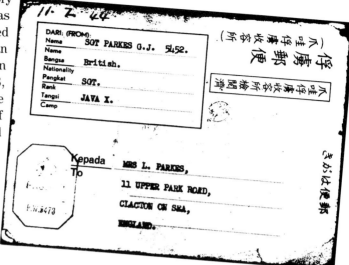

Official Japanese card sent by POW's to next of kin.

good news in banner headlines. Alongside the news of various thanksgiving services, and advertisements from local businesses, the Roll of Honour showed, to that date, 300 men from one small town had died .

An official announcement warned that VE Day celebrations would be low-key, 'there being no labour and few decorations.' This may have been the official view; the public thought otherwise and made decorations from anything available. Street parties were held, with people pooling rations to put on a decent spread. Giant bonfires were lit – despite warnings that the blackout was still in existence. Home Guard units and local sappers manufactured rockets, bangers and fireworks. At Walton-on-the-Naze, effigies of Hitler, Mussolini and Goering sat atop a bonfire. The effect was spoiled when an over-excited Home Guard threw a smoke canister into the fire. It spouted out thick clouds of bright red smoke, and set everyone coughing. Hitler, Goering and Mussolini blazed merrily, unseen.

Not all East Anglians were celebrating. Many had relatives either serving in the East or taken prisoner by the Japanese. It wasn't until after the dropping of the atomic bomb that their fate was known.

Gunner Frank Harwood of Walton-on-the-Naze was taken prisoner in the fall of Singapore. While being transported to Japan, his ship was torpedoed by the Allies. He survived 11 hours in the water before being re-captured. Of 386 prisoners on this ship, only 43 lived.

Harwood and his companions were taken to Nagasaki and forced to work in a Mitsubishi armaments factory – and were there when the atomic bomb was dropped.

"Air raids were, by now, quite common" Frank recalls. "On reaching the factory that particular morning, we were greeted by the sound of a siren which meant we had to return to the camp. Paraded in the compound, we were split into various details and sent to our dug-out shelters."

"The roof of the shelter was made of heavy reinforced concrete, but the strange thing about it was the series of holes and slots through which we could see the sky. I think perhaps, these vents had been incorporated into the original casting to allow light and air to circulate. A few minutes after taking cover, we heard the drone of approaching aircraft and peering up through the slots could hardly believe our eyes as wave after wave of bombers passed overhead, dropping their bombs. There was no opposition from Jap planes at all. How long the raid actually lasted is hard to say, but after the all-clear sounded. we were marched back to the factory. A couple of the factories had been hit, causing several casualties, but I couldn't say for sure if any of our POWs had been killed", remembers Frank.

"Back at the factory, there was very little in the way of actual work to be done, so we were put to cleaning up the bomb damage. It took the best part of two days to clear the workshop, but this was only the minor, light stuff. We were in no condition to tackle anything else. Then we marched back to our own camp to try and clear some of the debris from there."

"To carry out this task, we split into pairs. My partner was a Corporal Shore of the RAF. There seemed to be an awful lot of debris scattered around the living quarters and passageway, so we decided to try and clear this first. We had only got half way along this area when suddenly, we heard the sound of a solitary plane which sounded as if it was diving straight for us." (Many years later, Frank Harwood learned that the American B-29 flown by Major Sweeney hadn't actually dived when dropping the bomb, but had accelerated the engines, which gave the impression of a dive to those below, as the plane banked to avoid the cloud of dangerous A-bomb dust).

"Having just experienced the previous bombing raid, our one thought was to try and make for the safety of the shelters out in the compound. Corporal Shore being much younger than I, and in a slightly better state of health, managed to run down the passage and get outside. I knew it was a complete waste of time to even consider making a dash .... I just wasn't up to it. Looking for a place to shelter, in case the camp was hit again, I decided to take cover by the side of a large concrete water tank standing close by. Just as I threw myself under this, there was a terrific crack, like thunder, only many times louder, followed by a brilliant flash. I felt my whole body being sucked in by the force of the explosion then, almost immediately, experienced the strange feeling of expanding, rather like a rubber balloon."

"The entire wooden building collapsed around me. My back, legs and arms were badly cut and bruised by falling tiles and splintered timbers. The force of the explosion had jolted my head back against the base of the concrete water trough, causing me to black out. I have no idea how long I

Prisoners of war carved treenware, such as this peacock, using broken glass and scrap wood.

Left: *Frank Harwood before being posted to the Far East where he was captured. He is shown, right, with a pair of aluminium chopsticks found in the wreckage of a POW compound after the atomic attack on Nagasaki where he was a prisoner.*

was there, but recovering consciousness, I remember trying to clear a space among the debris so that I could stand upright. All that was left of the camp was piles of burning timber."

Frank Harwood eventually extricated himself from the ruins. Wandering, bedraggled and dazed from the scene, he witnessed many terrible sights. Men, women and children, burnt, blistered, wearing rags or naked, called out in vain for water. Making his way to the hills, Gunner Harwood looked down on Nagasaki and wondered what sort of weapon could have done so much damage.

Eventually, he was rescued by the Allies and despite tropical diseases and exposure to radiation, lived to tell the tale. Other returning East Anglian POWs were not as lucky as Frank. Disease and privation affected many of this "forgotten army" so badly that they were unable to work or lead normal lives ever again.

CHAPTER TWELVE
Mysteries and Secrets

*E*ven today, there is something mysterious and just a little unnerving about the Suffolk coast around Aldeburgh, Sizewell and Orford. During the war, this isolated region was the site of both mysteries and secrets, many not revealed until after the war; many still unexplained.

Being geographically close to occupied Europe, it was inevitable that the coast would enjoy a few close encounters with the Germans. But as well as being close to the Continent, the Ness area then was even more remote and isolated from the rest of Britain than it is today – the perfect location for developments that the Government was anxious to keep quiet.

Former Corporal James Arthur Wheeler, who served with the 2 nd/4 th Essex Regiment in the coastal area recalls a robbery by a thief who seemed to know what he was looking for.

"It was January 1940 when I and several other lads from my home town, were posted to Leiston, Aldeburgh, Thorpeness and Sizewell Hall to guard the beaches and marshes. There was always a fear that the Germans would launch their invasion along that stretch of coast. It was a thankless task – especially in the winter."

"Our regimental HQ was in a large old farmhouse, stuck in the middle of a field. The first Christmas we were there, some of the boys were set to guard the place – but being the festive season, they weren't very keen and all went off to the pub instead, leaving the place deserted. Next morning, there was the very Dickens to pay. Sometime during the night, somebody had walked into the Old Man's office and stolen his cash box. That didn't matter so much – what was really important was that he kept top secret plans of local defences and minefields in there with the regimental petty cash."

"Afterwards, several of the NCOs from the guard party were reduced to the ranks and one of the officers concerned found himself posted to a more active part of the war."

This wasn't the only strange thing to happen at that particular posting. George Wright, posted to the same place some months before the theft told of a strange "do" on a bleak winter night soon after his arrival.

George was a Corporal Wireless Operator. One of his jobs was to take hourly wireless reports from the various patrols scattered along the coast. One night late in December 1939, he lost contact with the Shingle Street squad. By 8 am the next morning, all the other patrols were back – but still no sign of the men from Shingle Street. By now, there was great concern for the safety of the missing men and a search party was despatched. Although the search was extended well beyond the normal patrol boundaries, all that was found was a rifle and a steel helmet near the water's edge.

No trace was ever found of the men, and the affair was hushed up. The general feeling was that the men had been taken by a patrolling submarine or E-boat, in the hope that they could give valuable information on some of the secret radar installations and defences along the coastline. If this was the case, what happened to them afterwards? Were they taken to a POW camp in Europe? Or, more likely, were they dropped over the side into the freezing waters of the North Sea once the Germans discovered that these ordinary rank and file infantrymen knew very little about such matters?

Another theory was that the ship or E-boat carrying the men was sunk by a patrolling British vessel. There is nothing in official records about the disappearance or fate of the men – but Observer Corps log books for that period make interesting reading ....

EXTRACT FROM OBSERVER CORPS NO 18 LOG BOOK

29th December, 1939, 1515 hrs. H2 (Orford) reports submarine close to land in (map ref) M8765 (close to Shingle Street and Hollesley Bay), and that two small boats had left the submarine.

21st February, 1940 ... H2 post again reports moaning sound at sea. Could be a submarine charging batteries, Harwich requests to be notified if sound returns. Explosions heard in location of sounds, 22.2.40.

Several patrols reported strange happenings, and a character known as Old Smokey Joe, who kept a tea shack near Sizewell may even have played host to a U-boat crew! Smokey Joe's shack was a Dickensian shanty, shrouded with canvas and a thick coating of black tar. Come the war, he enjoyed a brief period of prosperity catering for the shore patrols – later banned from using his facilities after several outbreaks of food poisoning.

According to Joe, a submarine was beached in a backwater creek during the first winter of the war. Some of the crew members took to calling at his hut for food and water. They told the old man that they were Dutch. Seeing no reason to disbelieve them, he didn't tell anyone about his "visitors" until well after the event!

With the foundation of the Third Reich in 1933, Hitler had begun to build a large and impressive air force. The Air Ministry saw this as an immediate threat, as Britain was within easy bombing range, so was anxious to develop a scientific weapon to detect incoming aircraft. With the Press clamouring for a "death ray", Watson Watt of the National Physical Laboratory was consulted to see if such as thing was possible. His view was that the quantity of energy needed to upset an engine or hurt a person was far too great to be provided by any then known method, but that the quantity of energy needed to detect the presence of aeroplanes or other objects might reasonably be produced by an extension of known means (*Science at War, J. G Crowther and R Whiddington*).

Watson Watt was given the green light to go ahead with his experiments, and, armed with a small van packed with radar receivers, was soon able to demonstrate the tracking of a lone aircraft some eight miles away. He was given the go-ahead, and a special laboratory was built at Orford Ness. He was soon able to demonstrate tracking up to 40 miles away when members of the Tizard Committee visited the site. By March 1939, the equipment was moved to larger premises at Bawdsey Manor near Felixstowe. Towers 250 ft high were built, and were able to track aircraft flying at 1500 ft, up to 75 miles away.

The observers at Bawdsey could follow the arrival of aircraft from Europe more accurately than the controller at Croydon Airport. One thing they did notice was that Deutsche Lufthansa aircraft nearly always flew low over Bawdsey when they approached or left England !

By May 1937, RAF officers were being trained to use the Bawdsey equipment for fighting operations. Work began on a chain of stations to cover the Thames Estuary. By the time Mr Chamberlain left for his fateful meeting in Munich, over £2,000,000 had been spent on the secret weapon and the east coast of Britain was cloaked by invisible radio waves. Aircraft travelling at 15,000 ft more than 100 miles away could be detected through rain, cloud, darkness or fog. Exact numbers could be counted and evading tactics observed and logged. Radio location techniques for directing anti-aircraft guns had also been perfected at Bawdsey, with the first gun-laying radio location equipment in service early in 1939. The first time radio location was used to control heavy guns in action was October 1940.

Local rumour concerning the "goings on" at Bawdsey was, of course, rife. Some motorists complained that vehicles suffered engine failure when approaching the area, especially if on high ground! Others complained that aircraft had "dropped like stones", also with engine failure when flying over or near the radar station. When the station was based at Orford Ness, a far more sinister complaint was made by fishermen who claimed that exposed parts of their bodies were being blistered by the rays. The authorities, of course, debunked all of these allegations with a liberal dose of official whitewash – even suggesting that the fishermen had been exposed to the wind and sun for too long! Who knows what was going on? Even today, the area remains cloaked in secrecy.

Tall radar masts were erected all over the region. Travellers using the A604 Harwich to Colchester road will notice the towering steel mast as they pass the Great Bromley turn off – the only remnant of the three masts built there early in the war. The entire area is honeycombed with deep bunkers and shelters, used for stores and personnel.

Former Special Police Constable, the late Frederick Dansie, was part of a team responsible for patrolling a 14-mile patch, allowing no one into the restricted zone unless they had a special pass. He recalls stumbling over a briefcase as he sought shelter in a pub doorway one stormy winter night. Inside were plans, maps and blueprints of the entire coastal radar network. Mr Dansie never did establish if the briefcase had been genuinely misplaced or "lost" intentionally for an enemy agent to pick up during the night.

No effort was spared to protect this important strip of coastline. Barbed wire fences, steel scaffolding and railway lines embedded in concrete on the low water line protected the beaches. The entire area was sown with land mines. In July 1940, the King visited Felixstowe, arriving by water from Harwich, to inspect the defences and 300-year-old Landguard Fort. He must have been impressed by the flame gun. In an attempt to repel invaders, a series of giant flame throwers had been built into strategically placed cliff faces around the coast. Fuel was supplied to the guns by oil tanks hidden on the cliff tops.

Whole areas of the east coast were equipped with these secret weapons, and it is rumoured that they were used during the early days of the invasion scare. Mr Arthur Tricker, an engineer stationed at Butlin's Holiday Camp, Clacton, remembers the time a party of Pioneers turned up at the camp with money to burn - unusual at a time when an ordinary serviceman had to exist on just a few shillings a week.

"I got talking to a three-striper, who told me that at their last posting, a camp near Great Yarmouth – he and his men had landed the job of breaching the barbed wire to drag in the bodies of several dozen Germans from below the low water mark. According to him, the bodies were fully equipped, but all badly burnt. He and his men were paid 2s 6d for every body they buried in a large, unmarked grave."

It was thought that these men may have been part of an invasion advance party, split from the main force and destroyed by the flame guns.

A number of other hush-hush projects were developed around East Anglia, including experiments with rockets on the Walton-on-the-Naze marshes overlooking Harwich harbour. Locals recall the time when the town was shaken to its foundations and the whole area lit by a strange phosphorescent glow that turned night into day when something "went off." Other secret projects developed in the area included the limpet mine and a

Remains of concrete bases built for the giant wooden radar masts at Great Bromley.

One of the deep reinforced concrete bunkers used to house radar personnel at Great Bromley.

rocket launcher capable of delivering 128 rockets from a large rack known as a projector.

During the early stages of the war, Britain's defences were heavily committed – so everyone was surprised when a number of submarines suddenly appeared around the Harwich/Brightlingsea/Walton-on-the-Naze area. The boats were built at Wivenhoe shipyard and were made entirely of wood. As dummies, they were convincing. Mr A G Bareham, a ships' carpenter remembers that the submarines were exactly like the real thing, right down to a wooden deck gun mounted on the bow.

Once afloat, the dummies were towed to their "bases" to take up a defensive position. The submarine shipped to Walton slipped its tow rope and was driven ashore into scaffolding defences at Holland-on-Sea. It must have looked realistic .... a few nights later, Lord Haw-Haw announced that "the submarine pens now being built at Holland-on-Sea will receive a visit from the Luftwaffe." Sure enough, a machine-gun raid was carried out within the week. Another time, a decoy sub lying off Harwich was attacked and the sentry, a straw filled dummy dressed in a sailor suit, was riddled with machine-gun bullets.

Submarines weren't the only decoy. One of the war's best kept secrets must be the building and staffing of decoy sites around East Anglia in an attempt to draw enemy bombing raids away from vital targets. This secret was so well kept that little was known about these sites until the 1960s. It was only after chatting to a former Intelligence Officer that I was given a clue that would lead to sites scattered around the region.

The idea of building decoy sites had been seriously considered since the start of the war, and was discussed in detail by Bomber Command throughout September 1939. By October of 1939, the man in charge of the project, Colonel John Turner, had established his workshop at Shepperton film studios where much of the construction work was undertaken.

By 1940, examples of dummy fields had been built. The country was divided into four areas, to initially house three dozen sites. Scotland, Northumberland and Durham were K1, Lincolnshire and Yorkshire K2, K4 the south east and K5 East Anglia and counties to the west with HQ at Mildenhall.

Known as Q, K and Drim sites, the original plan was to build decoys to cover airfields and important towns, ports and military installations. The Q sites, named after the decoy Q ships used during the First War World were built to resemble a dock or harbour. A K site had dummy aircraft, bomb and petrol dumps and a flare path, while the Drim site was usually a flare path equipped with a minimum of personnel.

Norwich was equipped with a decoy site, which during a Baedeker raid in 1942, received a load of incendiary bombs destined for the city. The port of Ipswich was covered by a decoy site built in a field on the north side of the

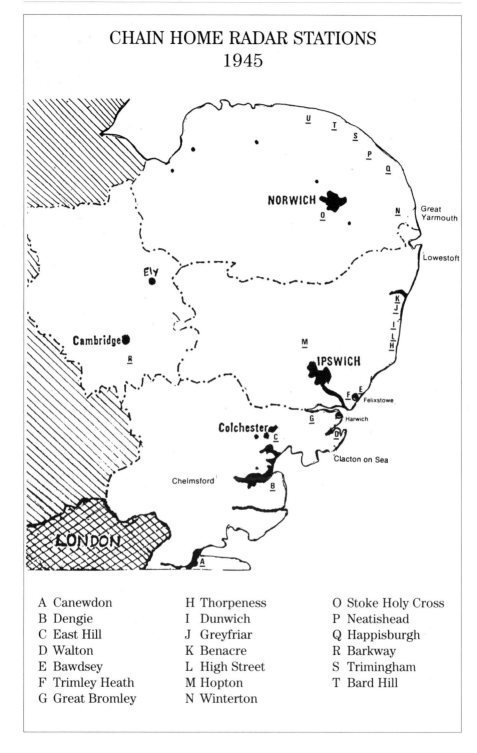

CHAIN HOME RADAR STATIONS
1945

A Canewdon	H Thorpeness	O Stoke Holy Cross
B Dengie	I Dunwich	P Neatishead
C East Hill	J Greyfriar	Q Happisburgh
D Walton	K Benacre	R Barkway
E Bawdsey	L High Street	S Trimingham
F Trimley Heath	M Hopton	T Bard Hill
G Great Bromley	N Winterton	

Ipswich to Felixstowe road, near the S-bend between Nacton crossroads and Levington Bridge. The officer in charge of this site had his Martello tower in the heart of Felixstowe. In here, with a battery of teleprinters and telephones, he would wait for the signal which would tell him to light up the decoy site and order the troops based in Ipswich to start making smoke to cover the town.

Although the Ipswich site was never officially used in anger, there was a practice run. One over-zealous officer wanted to see if the smoke troops (made up of conscientious objectors) were ready if the call came. The port of Ipswich soon vanished beneath a thick black cloud – only to have the wind change and blow the smoke into the town where the inhabitants spent the rest of the day coughing and spluttering!

Another Q site was built on the lower marshes near Shop Lane, East Mersea in 1940-41. Planned by the Admiralty, and built with civilian labour, its function was to cover the mine sweeper base at Brightlingsea. It was controlled by a squad of six men based in a pillbox, concealed by earth and bracken. The actual decoy buildings were made from wood and tubular steel, covered with thin canvas and thatching which allowed a glimmer of light to shine through when the unit was lit up at night. Lanterns were suspended on a rope near the water's edge to simulate marshalling yard lights on the move. Tanks of oil and water built on high gantries had been fitted with a remote-control mechanism, allowing both oil and water to flow into a series of shallow ditches. A small remote control bomb beneath the tanks could be detonated to light the mixture and the site, leading the enemy to believe that he had scored a direct hit.

Again, this site was never used in anger – but did once catch light, as Mersea Island decoy site guard, the late Hubert Inman, recalled.

"We didn't have much to do all day out there except to sit and watch the grass grow. In summer, the grass around the site was tall and wild. To make the place look occupied, we had to cut it with scythes. Unfortunately, our enthusiasm ran away with us, and we accidentally cut through a mass of wires used to control the lights and the explosive mechanism. We joined them up – but without the blueprint, we short-circuited the system and the whole place went up in a cloud of smoke and flames. It had to be rebuilt."

Other sites existed around East Anglia, at Walton-on-the-Naze marsh, built to cover the explosives factory on Bramble Island (where two men were killed trying to rescue a dog from a minefield), one at Great Bromley to cover Colchester railway station, and one at Bradfield. These Q sites were under the command of the late Lt Commander WAA Greenwell, RNVR, based at Harwich.

Most of the sites were guarded by heavy artillery, camouflaged to avoid enemy suspicions. The Ipswich site was guarded by a rail-mounted coastal defence gun, hidden in a copse of fir trees – at least it was hidden until a

Made from wood and canvas, decoy sites were uncannily like the real thing when viewed from the air.

A typical East Anglian Chain Home radar station.

series of practice fires denuded the trees in the area. Another gun close by remained hidden throughout the war, concealed in what looked like a farm store. The roof and upper half of the building were mounted on rails and could be slid back so that the gun could be elevated. Anyone interested can still see the building, without the extended rails, standing between the A45 and the railway on the Ipswich side of the road leading to Stratton Hall and the Suffolk Yacht Harbour.

During the early days, decoy aircraft were rather badly made and given to folding up and warping once exposed to the weather. Eventually, the manufacturers and designers, one a leading pre-war stage illusionist, hit on more substantial designs, supplied in kit form. A Wellington bomber cost £400, a Blenheim £150. The aircraft were painted in combat colours on site by RAF ground crew.

A K site was built on Cavenham Heath, near the villages of Tuddenham and Cavenham. The aircraft were Wellingtons. Drim sites were built at Littleport near Ely, and at Nacton.

As the war progressed, the Allies started to build up a concentration of arms and troops for the invasion. More decoy sites were built along the East Anglian coast to distract enemy attention from the real thing. In April 1944, a scheme code-named Fortitude South involved the creation of a million strong, 50-division decoy invasion force. In southern and south western England, Montgomery's 21st and Bradley's 12th army groups were being assembled. On D-Day, Montgomery would strike out for Normandy, and Bradley would follow once the beach head had been established. To try and make the Germans believe that a third force, the First United States Army Group was assembling in south eastern England to launch a major attack against the Pas de Calais, a series of dummy petrol dumps, sewage farms, hospitals, tank parks and barracks were constructed around East Anglia. Calculated leakages began to appear in the Press and on the wireless to foster this illusion.

During the Neptune build-up for D-Day, German aircraft were allowed to intrude into the FUSAG area. There, around harbours, river mouths and tiny creeks from Yarmouth to Lowestoft, the Broads, the Orwell and the Debden, they spotted over 400 "landing craft". Crews were made up of over-age or unfit soldiers from units of the 4th Northamptonshires and 10th Worcestershires. With motor boats fussing around, they gave the illusion of an invading force gathering strength.

With all this activity in one area, the presence of enemy agents lurking around the coast could not be ruled out. Two were captured landing on the Suffolk coast in the early days of the war. One agent was known to have spent his war around the Walton-on-the-Naze/Harwich area and was never caught. British Intelligence knew of the existence of most enemy agents and, in a number of cases, recruited them as double agents, allowing them to

GERMAN INVASION PLAN, 1939-1945

German plans for invasion were finalised in 1939.
There has been speculation that a small invading force was
repelled at Shingle Street, Suffolk - but the truth
may never be known.

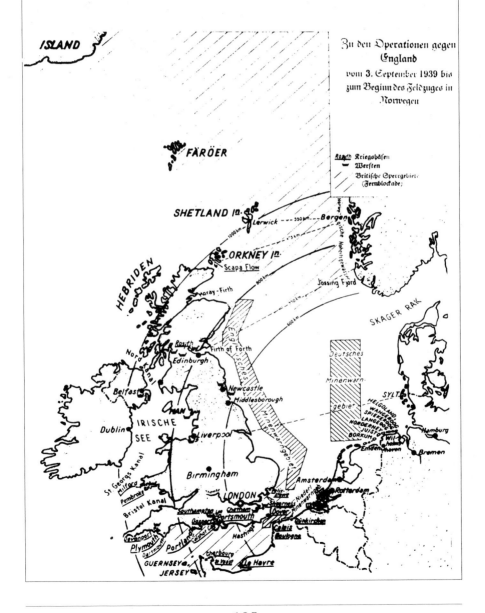

send snippets of both useful and useless information back to Germany. Sometimes, these XX agents, as they were known, fed back information the British wanted the Germans to know. In many cases, these agents could hardly speak proper English, let alone cope with money and ration books. One wonders if these apparently useless men were a blind for other, cleverer, better equipped spies.

Before the war, during the summers of 1938/39, private German aircraft, and aircraft of the Deutsche Lufthansa were suspected of taking photographs of almost every important town and city in the country. Listed together with details of pumping and electricity stations, hospitals, town halls, wireless masts and even early closing days, the efficient Teutonic mind had even included the known population of each place listed. The maps gave precise details of telegraph and telephone lines and water pumping stations; one even gave the geological breakdown of Britain. Youngsters from the Deutsches Jungvolk and Hitler Jugend on hiking and camping holidays listed and noted places of military and industrial interest. In some instances, when more detailed information was requested by Abwehr, British Union of Fascists sympathisers obliged with photographs.

East Anglia also played host to a special brand of British undercover agent. Acting as ARP, Observer Corps or, in one instance, as a member of the Civil Defence, these men and women were responsible for tracking and logging wireless messages in and out of Britain. With a wireless hidden in an innocent-looking suitcase, these agents monitored all recorded and unrecorded wireless traffic. Living in a twilight, make-believe world, they were also employed in relaying messages to partisan groups working behind enemy lines in Europe. They were used in tracking down wireless stations being used by British based enemy agents. Provided the spy stayed on the air long enough for the British operator to get a cross bearing on his set, the exact location could be pinpointed in a very short time.

Life was difficult for these undercover agents. They didn't work normal hours, or attend official duties, which gave rise to suspicion and hostile scrutiny. When this happened, the agent had to be moved. If unfortunate enough to be arrested, a phone call to a special number would result in release and removal from the district.

One of East Anglia's greatest wartime secrets, still classified information. revolves around the isolated village of Shingle Street. Tucked close to Hollesley Bay, lying between Bawdsey and Havergate Island bird sanctuary, Shingle Street is a long bar of sand and pebble, populated by a smattering of hardy inhabitants. At the beginning of the war, the owners of some 20 cottages were forced to leave their homes as the village was requisitioned for secret experimental work by British and American armaments experts. The inventor Barnes Wallis used the area for experimental bomb tests in 1940, during which the Shingle Street pub suffered a direct hit – much to his delight.

Inventor Barnes Wallis (centre) with men of the local fire brigade and police force during experimental bomb tests at Shingle Street.

The village of Shingle Street - still keeping some wartime secrets.

When the Ministry of Defence first announced that the contents of the War Government file on Shingle Street were not, as is usual, to be declassified and released to the Public Records Office after the normal 30 year span, national and local interest was aroused. The file, indexed Evacuation of the Civil Population from Shingle Street, Suffolk, earned itself a 75 year embargo with a ban on official publication of the contents until the year 2014.

When approached, an MOD spokesman said, "this has been classified for 30 years as Top Secret and, as we are not going to release it for another 45 years, you might say it remains Top Secret. This embargo usually only applies when it comes to something of national importance."

An official at the Public Records Office said that the embargo was extended at the request of a government department and with the approval of the Lord Chancellor. This was granted for reasons of national security, to protect confidential information supplied by members of the public, or where publication of records would distress or embarrass any living person.

So, what happened at Shingle Street?

Interviewing former members of the local police and coastguard produced very little – all gave the general impression, although unwilling to put it into words, that some-thing nasty had happened at Shingle Street in the war, during the war. One former coastguard readily admitted: "Yes, I know what happened at Shingle Street, but I can't afford to tell you anything as I'm still covered by the Official Secrets Act."

Eventually, I made contact with Miss Pierce Butler of Woodbridge, who during the war paid a brief visit to her cousin Lady Prestige of Bourne Park, Canterbury. Also

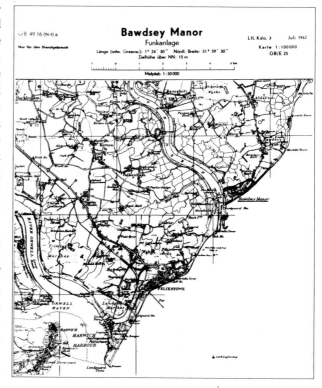

staying at Bourne Park was Air Commodore Patrick Huskinson. The Air Commodore, although blinded by flying glass when a bomb exploded in London, was kept on by the Department, working by touch alone. During her stay at Bourne Park, Miss Butler often accompanied the Air Commodore on fishing trips, acting as rower, guide and eyes. Learning that she originated from Shingle Street, he chanced to remark that tests of a very important nature were being carried out there on a revolutionary type of bomb, one that could change the course of the war.

I discovered a little more when approached by a former MI6 – MI9 operative who happened to live close to Shingle Street. He knew where most of the wartime decoy sites and various underground bunkers were located, and took me on a tour. During this tour he remarked, "I seem to recall hearing on the grapevine that some sort of experimental chemical warfare weapon had been developed around the Shingle Street/Sudbourne Marsh/Orford stretch of coast, and during the subsequent tests, an accident had occurred, resulting in a number of casualties."

It is a well established fact that the Allies had begun to manufacture a special biological bomb by 1943. Code named N, weighing 4lb and filled with anthrax spores, it was probably the greatest Allied secret of the war, next to the development of the atomic bomb. In the Public Record Office, there is a memo to Winston Churchill from Lord Cherwell, stressing the importance of stocking the N bomb.

Most Secret
PRIME MINISTER
N

Any animal breathing in minute quantities of these N spores is extremely likely to die suddenly but peacefully within the week. There is no known cure and no effective prophylaxis. There is little doubt that it is equally lethal to human beings.

N spores may lie dormant on the ground for months and perhaps years but can be raised to a very fine dust by explosions, vehicles or even people walking about.

Apparently, it is extremely difficult to get rid of once it has been scattered. Its use would consequently be well behind the lines, to render towns uninhabitable and indeed dangerous to enter without a respirator.

We have developed what we believe to be effective means of scattering and storing N spores in 4lb bombs which go into the ordinary incendiary containers. Half a dozen Lancasters could apparently carry enough, if spread evenly, to kill anyone found within a square mile and render it uninhabitable thereafter.

This was so secret, that the typist left blanks where the words 'N spores' appear for Lord Cherwell to fill in by hand.

Churchill's response was to order half a million bombs ... "we should regard this as a first instalment", he noted.

Yet another chemical warfare weapon tested over the east coast was a defoliating compound. As early as 1940, researchers at ICI had perfected a number of substances showing growth retarding properties. They had discovered two anti-crop chemicals, one called 1313 which acted against crops like barley, rye, wheat and oats, and 1414 which acted against root crops.

Aerial spray tests were carried out over this region during the early years of the war, and it is a recorded than an anthrax bomb was exploded on a remote beach in Wales.

Following increased media interest and pressure from local MPs, the file was opened ahead of time in summer 1992. It proved to contain little of interest – other than some details of mustard gas testing. There were no details of any invasion, "friendly fire" incident or of bodies being washed up on the beach. It seems likely that "sensitive" material was removed before the file was opened – so the mystery of Shingle Street remains a mystery.

CHAPTER THIRTEEN
On the Home Front

War, does not of course, affect only those at the front. For those left at home, the years between 1939 and 1945 brought many changes, and many hardships. What was life like for those left behind in East Anglia when the men went off to war? Not easy for the wife of a private soldier who was expected to keep a home and bring up two young children on just 25s (£1.25) a week plus 7s (35p) stopped from her husband's pay. Not that there was much to buy with the money, had it been available as everything was in short supply. When rationing came into force on January 8, 1940, civilians were allowed four ounces of ham or bacon a week, four ounces of butter and twelve ounces of sugar. Meat rationing started in March, with 1s 10d worth (about 9p) a week for those over six, and 11d (5p) for smaller children. The adult ration was eventually reduced to 1s 1d (about 5¹/₂p). Worst of all for the tea-loving British was the introduction of tea rationing. Adults were allowed just two ounces of tea a week. By 1940, family store cupboards were almost bare. Tins of fruit, dried fruit, biscuits and tinned fish had all but vanished from the shops. Housewives spent hours queing in the hope of buying just about anything. One King's Lynn housewife recalled the time when she stood for an hour and a half to find that all that was left was a couple of fly papers. "I didn't know what they were selling", she said. "But I thought that if there was a queue, it must be for something worthwhile. I bought them not because I needed them, but to justify the time spent in the queue." Times were, indeed, hard for housewives.

Family pets, used to a peaceful life, fled in terror at the sound of the first sirens. Sometimes they would run for miles, until dropping from sheer exhaustion, the poor animals hid in sheds or cellars for days on end. Frightened and far from home, these animals wandered the streets until taken into care and ultimately destroyed. RSPCA figures for the first fortnight of the war list something like 200,000 dogs being destroyed. Pets were not officially allowed in public shelters. Those who didn't fancy leaving their dog or cat to take its chances could buy a gas-proof kennel from the PDSA for £4. Norfolk landowners with the necessary funds could send their gun dogs off to the peace and quiet of good old Donegal for £1 a week. Other dogs cost 10s (50p). Alongside the list outside houses detailing the number of inhabitants (so that the rescue services would know how many bodies to look for after a raid) another small ticket issued by the Canine Defence League listed family dogs. A scheme was introduced to find a home for dogs left behind by soldiers. If the dog was young or fit enough, it could always join up – as this appeal from the RSPCA shows.

'The RSPCA urgently requires more dogs for active service with the British Army. They are: alsatians, Airedales, lurchers, collies and crosses between them, bull terriers, elk hounds, Himalayan sheep dogs, Rhodesian ridgebacks, being over nine months old and under six years of age.'

Although people living in rural East Anglia were able to heat their homes using wood, and could rely on fresh produce from gardens and farms, life was harder for those living in Norwich, Ipswich and nearer London. Fuel was short and it became common practice for city dwellers to bring a lump of coal if invited for an evening out. The harsh winter of 1940 saw town folk making their own fuel by mixing coal dust with wet cement to form bri-quettes, and sawdust with glue to make evil-smelling 'logs'. The authorities tried to encourage householders to burn coke which was obtainable from the gasworks and rationed to 28 lb per person. Women queued for hours, armed with battered prams, wheelbarrows and sledges to carry the fuel home. Even bombing raids had their compensations as shattered timber was piled in a central depot where people could help themselves.

Candles and torches vanished from the shops. Those living in rural East Anglia simply revived old crafts, making candles from animal fats and beeswax with a wick hand-rolled from tow or hemp. Oil for lamps was extracted from rape seed. Even sheep wool was collected from the hedges and spun into yarn – nothing, in the old country tradition, went to waste.

Throughout the war, civilians suffered a deluge of restrictions, regulations and reductions. Clothes rationing, introduced in June 1941, was keenly felt by women. As shortages of clothing became worse, many took to wearing the Churchillian siren suit, a baggy overall with front zip and a pixie-type hood. From June 1942, it was illegal to manufacture bedspreads or table-cloths. Blankets and sheets were only available to newly-weds or victims of bombing. Make do and mend became a way of life for everyone. Flour sacks were washed, dyed and used as curtains, blankets, and with pieces of coloured rag threaded through, served as a durable, if rather rustic, flooring. Oil cloth and lino disappeared – replaced by heavy-duty roofing felt painted and tacked to the floorboards.

The British public had very little to laugh about, with nothing to eat, little

Women turned to all sorts of occupations formerly exclusive to men – as these FANY motor mechanics demonstrate.

Members of the WVS building an emergency field kitchen after a bombing raid on Norwich.

to wear and daily bombings. Nevertheless, people tried to remain cheerful – with little help from the film industry which showed a selection of government exhortations, low-budget American productions and propaganda-inspired dramas with stiff upper lip British heroes. In East Anglia, many cinemas were forced to close, owing to Government restrictions and lack of audience, but as troops began to move in, the rules were relaxed and queues waited to see such epics as *Come On George* and *Goodbye Mr Chips*. On excursions to the pictures, sweets and ice cream were, of course, off. Even the heating was either very low or non-existent so cinema-goers took hot water bottles and Thermos flasks

William Joyce – better known as Lord Haw-Haw.

with them for an evening's viewing. A warning was flashed on the screen if there was an air raid during the showing. After the initial panic, most audiences decided to sit it out. As one Walton resident remarked: "We reckoned that if we were going to be hit, then let's go while we are enjoying ourselves."

At home, civilians could enjoy the gramophone or the wireless. The wireless did much to keep wartime spirits buoyant. Various comedy programmes such as *Mind My Bike, Can You Hear Me Mother, Band Waggon* and request shows such as *Sandy's Half Hour* were regular listening. *ITMA* was probably the most popular of all the wartime radio programmes, and spawned a collection of catch-phrases such as TTFN (ta-ta for now) and "Can I do you now sir?" Lord Haw-Haw, with his broadcasts from Germany was almost as popular as the comedies. He often mentioned East Anglian towns and villages and had an uncanny knowledge of events. His information came from the Luftwaffe and the German spy network.

The wireless was also used to relay information on making the most of rations. Frederick Grisewood and Mabel Constanduros were stars of *The Kitchen Front*, broadcasting recipes such as Woolton Pie devised by the Ministry of Food. Women found themselves cast in a new role during the war years. No longer was a woman's place in the home. It was in the factories, on the buses and in the rescue services instead. By autumn 1943, 100,000 women were working on the railways, serving and trained in 250 different grades. In other fields, women turned their hands to almost anything from window cleaning to munitions. Engineering and munitions were the most popular of female occupations. Women started work at Ford in Dagenham in 1941. By the time of the Japanese surrender in 1945, 2217 women were working on the assembly lines. They worked extremely hard, carrying out tasks previously believed to be exclusive to men. Most of the women at Ford worked on the assembly lines and were from all walks of life. They took welding, moulding, machining and finishing malleable castings in their stride. Because more than 2000 women refused to wear the official mob-cap, machines had to be fitted with an intricate system of safety guards to prevent long hair from being caught in the workings.

Women of conscription age were offered a choice between the Forces, munitions or other essential work, or the Land Army. Many country girls chose the WAAF or ATS as a chance to escape the rustic life and see something of the world

FOOD FACTS
Number 37

Making the most of the MILK

FROM April 13th onwards your milk supply will be reduced by about one seventh. The reason for this is that the Ministry of Food has to look ahead and put aside in the National Larder supplies of food that will keep for the winter when everyone needs more to eat.

The milk that is saved will be made into cheese and tinned milk for store.

There will be no reduction in supplies to mothers and children under the National Milk Scheme, to children in schools or to hospital patients.

HOW THE PLAN WILL WORK

Your milkman will tell you by how much you should reduce your weekly purchases in order that you may play your part in this important contribution to the national store cupboard. You should arrange with him to make the reduction in the way most convenient to you both. Remember that it is his job to give everyone a fair share. If you are moving, and have to change your milkman, be patient if you do not get your proper supplies for a day or two.

Try to arrange for your delivery of milk to be shared out among the members of your family according to their needs. Let a temporary invalid, for instance, have a little more by giving the others a little less.

In certain cases of illness where milk is particularly necessary, doctors can authorise extra supplies by completing a form of certificate which will be obtainable at any Local Food Office.

GOOD NEWS ABOUT BREAD

When we have to face a minus in our milk, it is specially welcome to find a plus somewhere else. Here it is — in bread! National Wheatmeal Bread has been called quite rightly the *plus* bread. It contains the vital "germ" of the wheat. National Wheatmeal Bread is better in flavour, in texture, in keeping, and in real nutritive goodness. There aren't many things that are better in war-time — but here is one of them! Take advantage of it! And if you find any difficulty in getting it from your baker, write to the Ministry of Food about it. You will never regret the stamp or the trouble. This is the address:

THE MINISTRY OF FOOD, LONDON, S.W.1

outside East Anglia. It was not just working and servicewomen who devoted time and energy to the war effort. In Norwich, Mrs Ruth Hardy became the organiser of a group called the Mutual Aid Good Neighbour's Association. The body was planned along the lines of the ARP and an appeal was launched for 2000 street organisers, 80 post organisers, twelve group leaders and three divisional heads. The prime aim of the group was to try and save the lives of people suffering from the effects of shell or bomb shock. Members offered shelter, sympathy and understanding and raised funds by running dances, concerts and whist drives. Over 30,000 women joined MAGNA; their yellow posters announcing "a good neighbour lives here." could be seen around the city.

No story of civilians at war would be complete without mentioning the WVS. Wherever there was a need for help, you could be sure that the WVS would be there with practical help, advice and comfort.

The Women's Volunteer Service was first thought of in spring 1938, when the Home Secretary, Sir Samuel Hoare, had contacted the Dowager Marchioness of Reading with the idea of forming an organisation to recruit women into the ARP. During those early days, the authorities believed that women were gentle creatures, in need of shelter from harsh realities, so recordings of bombs falling, used during practice exercises, were muted so as not to upset the ladies! By the end of 1938, the WVS had attracted 32,329 volunteers, all trained to live by their slogan – "The WVS never says no."

Their contribution during the war years was invaluable. They carried out a wide range of tasks, including helping householders to gas-proof their homes, gathering salvage, raising funds and assisting bombed-out families. The true test of their mettle came with the evacuation. During the first three days of September 1939, one and a half million people were evacuated. The WVS supervised the movement of children, organised food and drinks along the way, helped with billeting and collected blankets, mattresses and clothing for the poorer children. When the bed-wetting problem reached astronomical proportions, WVS members spent hours stuffing canvas paliasse covers with straw.

Improvisation was the order of the day for the ladies in green. Desperate for material to make children's clothing and sheets, they issued an appeal for plan drawings on linen. Boiled until soft and free from their paper covering, these drawings provided the perfect material for hospital supplies and baby clothes. Flour bags (then made from a hessian-type material), were converted into tea cloths – or shorts for smaller members of the local Cadet force. The WVS cut old stockings into strips for knitting into blankets – left-over snippets were used to stuff pillows.

With shortage of food a constant problem, the WVS held regular cookery demonstrations showing how to make the best of the limited supplies available and how to deal with formerly unknown fare such as whale meat, salted

cod, fat bacon and the dreaded soya sausages known as soyalinks. Later, street parties were held to demonstrate and popularise using jacket potatoes – felt to be more nutritious than the peeled version as the skin contains fibre and vitamins. As gas and electricity was often cut off during raids, the WVS were great demonstrators of the hay box, one of the oldest methods of cooking known to mankind. People were encouraged to keep rabbits, chickens and pigs and to grow vegetables. The allotment movement boomed!

Isolated searchlight batteries relied on the WVS mobile canteens for cheer and comfort. A Spalding WVS driver set out on a tour of Britain's bleakest marshes, to visit the troops. Named 'The Florence Nightingale of the marshes' by grateful soldiers, she drove her camouflaged van through bad weather and the blackout travelling up to 50 miles a day, six days a week. One half of the van was fitted out as a canteen for selling tea and cakes. The other half was a shop, stocked with all manner of goods, ranging from birthday cards to hair cream. In its first 14 weeks of operation, the vehicle travelled over 4000 miles, selling 20,000 cups of tea and 37,000 cakes.

The Government soon decided that a larger scale operation was needed to feed people after heavy bombing raids. The answer was the Queen's Messenger Convoy, consisting of two food storage lorries, two equipment lorries, four motor cycles, one water bowser and three mobile canteens. The convoy was staffed by a team of 50 mainly female volunteers. This scheme eventually led to the formation of the Mobile Emergency Feeding Units equipped with a collapsible shed, furniture, a solid fuel burner, a store of fuel, water and food and essential items of crockery. Companies such as Ford and Cadbury had welfare vans dispensing cocoa, tea and hot food to rescue workers.

WVS hostels were introduced for servicewomen and for the wives and girl-friends of servicemen stationed in the area. A special Polish hostel and can-teen was built in Cambridge for Polish ATS girls who had escaped from Poland during the early part of the war. It was a home from home for them, with English lessons, Slav music and song and Polish books.

Work carried out by the WVS infiltrated all levels of British society – wherever you went, the WVS were sure to be helping, organising, feeding and caring for the war-battered public. When Mrs Roosevelt played a flying goodwill visit late in the war she was shown, among many other things, an exhibition in Cambridge demonstrating the work of the WVS. This included book binding for the Forces Mobile Library; making toys and doll's houses for nurseries; carpet slippers for rest-centres; sniper suits; furniture for AA and searchlight huts and leather jackets for minesweeper crews. One of the most difficult jobs was making camouflage netting. With the coarse material spread out on trestles, the women crawled on hands and knees beneath it, weaving in strips of green and brown scrim. Altogether, 129,558 nets were made by the WVS for the Ministry of Supply.

East Anglian members of the WI worked closely with the WVS throughout the war years. The WI Country Herb Committee was set up by the Ministry of Supply in 1942 to organise the collection of medicinal herbs from the countryside. In small villages across East Anglia, WI members organised bands of children to collect bundles of nettles, foxgloves, raspberry leaves and rose hips. the youngsters were paid 1½d a bundle for the leaves and 3d a pound for rose hips and conkers. At Great Bentley, one of the Essex pack-ing stations, Mrs Athill and Mrs Burgess prepared the bundles of leaves for dispatch by rail to the chemical factories. The rose hips were made into a syrup, rich in Vitamin C, which was issued to mothers and babies. The conkers went to make tannic acid for creams and lotions used in the treat-ment of burns. Sorting and preparing the leaves, nuts and berries took great patience and care.

Not all wartime jobs undertaken by women were quite so straightforward and domestic. A little-publicised group was reponsible for manning the net-work of Home Guard underground wireless communications. Their work involved relaying coded messages and listening in to other wireless traffic. Buried deep within the confines of a damp bunker or cellar, these women spent long hours alone throughout the war years; their identities and true vocation known to just a handful of staff officers.

CHAPTER FOURTEEN

Glossary

AIR BASES OF EAST ANGLIA

ESSEX

Boreham
Used 1943–44 by the 349th Bomb Group flying B-26 bombers. Actual operations began in March 1944. The station closed for active duty in 1945.

Boxted
Opened in May 1943. The first Squadron was the 386th Bomb Group, flying B-26 bombers against enemy aerodromes in France.

Bradwell Bay
Now the site of a nuclear power station. Opened as an air base in 1941, and often used by returning planes needing fuel. Used by Canadians of 418 Squadron from 1942. Closed, 1945.

Chipping Ongar
Used largely by American forces, this base was built by them in 1942–43, coming into operational use in June 1943 when the 387th Bomb Group arrived with B-26s. Handed over to the RAF and army at the end of the war.

Debden
Debden was established in the 1930s. It was officially opened in April 1937, and 87 Squadron, flying Gladiators, was the first to take up residence. The station became an important fighter base, with many pilots taking part in the Battle of Britain. During 1940, the base was badly damaged by enemy raiders. Later, American and Canadian units saw action from Debden.

Earl's Colne
Opened by the RAF in 1942 but built by the US Army. May 1943 saw the arrival of the American 94th Bomb Group flying B-17s. They were replaced by the 323rd Bomb Group flying B-26s. In September 1944, 296 and 297

Squadrons of 38 Group took over the station, flying Albermarles and the Halifax IIIs. The station was closed as an operational airfield in 1946.

Gosfield

Opened 1943. The Americans took command in October with the 365th Fighter Group flying P-47s. They acted as fighter support for B26 Groups over France. Later, the 410th Bomb Group flying A-20s moved in to attack V-rocket sites and coastal targets. Closed, 1945.

Great Dunmow

Opened 1943 when the 386th Bomb Group arrived in their B-26s. The RAF then arrived with 190 and 620 Squadrons, equipped with Stirling IV bombers to test Horsa gliders for the planned crossing of the Rhine. Last official operation, 1945.

Great Saling

Better known as Andrewsfield, named after Lt General F M Andrews in 1943. This field was the first to be built by the US Pioneer Corps. First arrival was the 95th Bomb Group and their B-17s.

Great Sampford

Opened April 1942, closed August 1944. Used by 65 Squadron and Spitfire VBs of 616 Squadron. Later, American Eagle Squadrons joined the strength. Operational flights stopped in 1943 when the station was taken over by the RAF Regimental Battle School.

Little Walden

Opened for full operational use in March 1944 as Station 195 of the 8th USAF. Four squadrons of the 4409th (L) Bomb Group, flying A-20 Havocs and Mustangs of the 361st Fighter Group were based here. Later B-17s of the 493rd Bomb Group lodged at Little Walden for a short while. The base was closed in January 1946.

Matching

Started operations in 1944 with B-26s of the 391st Bomb Group carrying out raids against V-rocket sites. Taken over by the RAF and phased out in 1945.

Raydon

Leading fighter base built by the US Army. In 1943 the 357th Fighter Group arrived with their P-51s. In 1944, the 353rd arrived with P-47s used in low-level bombing raids on prime targets. Handed over to the RAF at the end of the war.

Ridgewell
Three-runway field opened in 1942 and operational in 1943 with Stirling bombers of 90 Squadron. Later, B-17Fs of the 381st Bomb Group took command. Taken over by the RAF at the end of the war.

Rivenhall
Opened in 1943 by the US 9th Air Force but not operational until February 1944 when the 363rd Fighter Group started operations flying P-51s. The 397th Bomb Group arived next. Up to the end of the war, Rivenhall was the base for 38 Group RAF and 295 and 570 Stirling IV transport squadrons.

Stansted
This major airport started life in 1942 as a 2000 acre airfield used by the 344th Bomb Group flying B-26s. Many daylight raids against occupied Holland and Belgium were flown from this base. Handed back to the RAF at the end of the war.

Wethersfield
Established in 1941 but not opened until January 1944 when Bomber Command took over. A month later, the USAAF 416th Bomb Group flying A-20Gs arrived. Later RAF Stirling IVs and the 9th Air Force with C-47s moved in. In the post-war years, this base played an important part in the NATO defence plan.

SUFFOLK BASES

Beccles
Built in 1943 for the USAAF and taken over by Bomber Command in 1944. Mosquitoes of 618 Squadron, Barracudas, Warwicks, Walruses and anti-submarine patrols by 810 Squadron were flown from this base.

Bentwaters
Originally known as Butley, this field was started in 1942, but the name was changed in 1943. Taken over by the RAF for Mustangs. Handed to the Americans in the 1950s.

Bungay
Opened in 1942 for B-24Ds of the 329th Bomb Squadron. In 1943 the 466th Bomb Group arrived with B-24Hs to carry out raids against the U-boat base at Kiel. Closed in 1945.

Chedburgh
Short Stirling bombers, Halifax C VIIIs and Lancasters flew from this station which opened in September 1942 and closed in 1946.

Debach
Built in 1943–44 by the US Army, this station was the last to house bombers of the 8th Air Force. Badly built, this field was frequently under repair causing aircraft to use other bases.

Eye
Built in 1944 and used by bombers of the 480th for strikes against Berlin, Hamburg and Munster. Closed at the end of the war.

Felixstowe
Originally established during the First World War, Felixstowe was used for testing various craft including the Sunderland, London, Iris, Stranraer and the six-engined Sarafand. During the war, this seaplane base was taken over by Coastal Command.

Framlingham
The 95th Bomb Group arrived in May 1943 to a base dogged by misfortune. During one of the first air strikes over Germany, almost half the force was lost to fighters. Later B-17s of the 390th Bomb Group arrived to carry out raids on German targets. The local population will always remember the Americans, especially Christmas 1944 when a heavily-laden aircraft failed on take off and dived into Parham, damaging every house in the village when the bomb load exploded. None of the villagers was injured, but the pilot and crew were killed. The base closed in 1945.

Great Ashfield
Opened in 1943, home of the 385th Bomb Group flying B-17s bombing France, Germany, Norway, Poland and Belgium.

Halesworth
Opened by the Americans in 1943 for P-47s of the 56th Fighter Group. Later, the 489th Bomb Group, flying B-24s, arrived to take part in softening up raids before the invasion. During the latter part of the war B-17s and P-51s operated from this base. It was taken over by the RAF in 1945.

Honington
Opened in 1937. Used by Wellingtons of 9 Squadron in the first bombing raid against enemy warships. Also played an important part in the 1000-bomber raid on Cologne. Later, the Americans moved in with B-17s of the 3rd Air Division and P-38Js of the 364th Fighter Group.

Horham
Another important American station used by the 47th, 95th and 323rd Bomb Groups. The 95th had the distinction of being the first 8th Air Force group to blitz Berlin. Taken over by the RAF in 1945.

Ipswich
Opened by the Prince of Wales in 1930 as official HQ of the Suffolk Aero Club. During the war it was used for target-towing and as a drop-off base for visiting fighter squadrons.

Knettishall
Opened in January 1943 for bombers of the 388th, flying targets against Holland and Germany.

Lakenheath
Came into operational use in 1941 and was used by 149 Squadron for mine-laying sorties.

Lavenham
Built between 1943 and 44 and used by the 487th Bomb Group, flying against targets in Nuremburg, Hamm, Mannheim and Berlin. Returned to the RAF.

Leiston
A famous Mustang fighter base taken over by the 358th Group in 1943 for long-range raids into the heart of Germany.

Martlesham Heath
Opened during the First World War as an Aeroplane Experimental Unit, this base became famous during the war as a top secret testing ground. Played an important part in the Battle of Britain with aircraft patrolling the east coast to protect convoys against enemy attack, plus serving as an air-sea rescue back up. The Americans also flew from Martlesham.

Mendlesham
The RAF arrived in 1943, followed by 310, 312 and 313 Czech Spitfire squadrons in 1944. The 34th Bomb Group also arrived in 1944. Used as an ammunition dump at the end of the war.

Mildenhall
King George V took the Silver Jubilee Review here in 1935. Between the wars, Heyfords and Fairey Hendons could be seen lumbering across the strip. Wellingtons of 149 Squadron took their place during the war. Both New Zealand and Canadian squadrons were posted here.

Newmarket Heath
Wartime home of Wellington and Stirling bombers, this famous station also flew Whitleys of 138 (Special Duty) Squadron on secret missions behind enemy lines. In 1943, a radar training unit was established here, plus a unit developing new bombing techniques.

Rattlesden
Taken over by the USAAF in 1942. B-26 Marauders flew from this base. In 1943, the 477th Bomb Group arrived to fly against V-rocket sites. Returned to the RAF in 1945.

Rougham
Opened in 1942, and used by the 322nd Bomb Group flying Marauders. In 1943, the 94th Bomb Group moved in to fly against tactical targets and German factories. Taken over by the RAF in 1945.

Shepherd's Grove
Built for the USAAF in 1943 and used by the RAF to fly Stirlings. No.s 196 and 299 Stirling IV transport squadrons operated from this base, carrying out SOE operations behind the lines and towing gliders for landing in Germany.

Stradishall
Pre-war station opened in 1938. The first aircraft based here were Heyford III's and Wellesleys. Wellingtons and Stirlings also flew from here. Stradishall was bombed on several occasions.

Sudbury
Short-lived field which saw the 486th Bomb Group take over in 1944, flying B-24s against important targets in Germany.

Tuddenham
Opened in October 1943. Stirlings of 90 Squadron flew from here. Later used for Lancasters.

Wattisham
A pre-war airfield opened in 1939, Wattisham became the home of 107 Squadron. Flying Blenheims, they participated in bombing raids on enemy naval targets in the first week of the war. In 1942, the Americans took over the base for the duration of the war with units of the 68th Observation Group and 479th Fighter Group.

Westley
Built in 1938 for the West Suffolk Aero Club and brought into operational service in 1941 when 241 Squadron moved in flying Lysanders. Auster training squadrons used the base until the end of the war.

Woodbridge
Opened during winter 1942, catering mainly for aircraft in distress, the strip was 2 miles in length and 250 yards wide with large grass overshoots. Close to the coast, it was a useful haven for planes too crippled to reach home base.

NORFOLK

Attlebridge
105 and 88 Squadrons moved in soon after this grass strip was opened to traffic in summer 1941. Bostons and Blenheims were in action over coastal regions. Later the American 319th Bomb Group took over.

Bircham Newton
Bircham Newton was used as a training school in 1916. In 1939, 206 Squadron took over, flying Ansons on coastal patrols, together with 42 Squadron. Part of their duties was to protect the herring fleet sailing from the Norfolk and Suffolk coasts. Weather reconnaisance was carried out by 403 Metereological Reconnaissance Flights.

Bodney
Opened 1940 with Blenheims of 82 Squadron. Others flying from Bodney were 352 Fighter Group. Closed late 1945.

Coltishall
Originally planned as a bomber station, Coltishall eventually became a fighter base in 1940 when 66 Squadron moved in. Other units using this field were 257 Squadron, 151 Defiant Squadron, 133 Eagle Squadron and Mosquitoes of 307 Squadron.

Deopham
The American 4252 Bomb Group took over in 1944 and was part of the 2000-plane raid on Berlin later that year. They sustained severe losses in this operation. Closed, summer 1945.

Docking
Opened in 1940 to Hudsons of 206 Squadron and later, Blenheims of 2325 Squadron. Spitfires, Beaufighters, Whitley VIIs and Hampden torpedo bombers operated from here. During the latter part of the war, Docking was used by Coastal Command units.

Downham Market
218 Squadron, flying Stirlings were the first to operate from this base in August 1942. 608 Mosquito Squadron also flew from here. Closed at the end of the war.

East Wretham
Primarily a bomber base, used mainly by Wellingtons and Lancasters of 311 and 115 Squadrons.

Feltwell
Opened for service in 1937 when 214 Squadron took over. Wellingtons of 37 Squadron and 3 Lancaster Finishing School were both there.

Fersfield
A top secret field, best remembered for USAAF and USN experiments involving radio-controlled flying bombs and the ill-fated Operation Aphrodite in which Joseph Kennedy Jnr was killed. Closed 1945.

Great Massingham
No. 18 Squadron took over in 1940 and later, Blenheims of 107 Squadron followed by Bostons of 342 Squadron moved in. In 1944, 1692 Bomber Support Training Flight, flying Beaufighters moved in.

Hardwick
Opened in 1942 for the 310th Bomb Group flying B-25 Mitchells. Later the 93rd with the B-24D took over to fly against targets in Germany and Italy.

Hethel
The 320th Bomb Group and 389th flew from here. Taken over by 65 Squadron after the war.

Horsham St Faith
Built as a bomber airfield and opened in 1940 when 264 Squadron flying Defiants moved in. Active throughout the war, especially after the arrival of the 319th Bomb Group in 1942. In 1944, B-24s of the 458th Bomb Group moved in flying missions in support of the second front. Handed back to the RAF in 1945.

Langham
Opened in 1940 for No. 1 Anti-Aircraft Co-operation Unit. Swordfish of 819 Squadron arrived in 1942 to carry out torpedo raids against enemy shipping. Wellingtons of 524 Squadron, Beaufighters of 455 and 489 were also stationed there. Closed in 1946.

Little Snoring
One of the first arrivals in 1943 was 115 Squadron flying Lancasters . Later that year, 169 and 515 Squadrons moved in with Blenheims and Beaufighters.

Ludham
Opened as a fighter base in 1941. Planes from 19 and 610 Squadrons operated convoy patrols and escorted bombers. In 1945, 91 Squadron flew in with Spitfire Mk XXIs. Closed 1945.

Marham
Originally known as Narborough, this station dates back to the First World War when it was opened in 1915 for anti-enemy airship patrols. Re-opened in 1937 as a bomber station for Wellingtons operated by 38, 218, 115 and 105 Squadrons.

Matlaske
Spitfires of 72 Squadron operated from this new field during the autumn of 1940. Spitfire VBs, Westland Whirlwind fighters, Lysanders, Walruses and American Mustangs all flew from here. Closed 1945.

Methwold
Used by Wellingtons of 37 Squadron followed by 214 Squadron, Ventures of 487 Squadron and Lancasters of 218 Squadron.

North Creake
Opened during the winter of 1943 for Lancasters and Wellingtons of 199 and 171 Squadrons. Closed at the end of the war.

North Pickenham
B-24s of the 492nd Bomb Group took over in spring 1944, flying behind-the-line missions and bombing coastal targets.,

Old Buckenham
Another American base used by Liberators of the 453rd Bomb group flying sorties against German targets. Closed at the end of the war.

Oulton

Opened in 1940 and used by 114 Squadron. Aircraft dropping in included Bostons, Mitchells and Fortresses.

Pulham

Home of the Pulham Pigs (airships, including the ill-fated R101), this former base was not used as an active airfield during the war. Instead, its buildings and storerooms served as munitions repositories. Pulham is best remembered as a dumping ground for 'pranged' aircraft from both enemy and Allied forces. Towards the latter part of the war, it was a common sight to see groups of Italian POWs helping to dismantle various wrecked planes for useful spare parts.

Rackheath

B-24s of the 467th Bomb group arrived at this airfield early in 1944 to take part in raids against Osnabruck, Keil, Hamm and Stuttgart. They sustained heavy losses in less than a year.

Sculthorpe

Built in 1942, Sculthorpe started out as a RAF station during the winter of 1943. Used at first for storage then taken over by 342 Free French Squadron equipped with Boston IIIs. 464 and 487 Squadrons moved in, flying Mosquito FB VIs. In 1944, the Americans arrived with B-17Fs. Re-opened for American bombers in the 1950s.

Seething

Built for the Americans, this field started operations in 1943 with the 448th Bomb Group flying Liberators. Credited with over 250 missions, the 448th took part in raids against prime German targets including a ball bearing factory in Berlin and an aircraft factory in Rostock. The Group made its last raid in April 1945.

Shipdham

Recorded as the first American heavy bomber station in Norfolk, Shipdham opened in 1942 for the arrival of the 219th Bomb Group (Medium). Their place was taken by the 44th, flying B-24Ds. They suffered heavy losses during early raids on targets such as Keil.

Snetterton Heath

Opened in 1943 to the 96th Bomb Group flying B-17s. The 96th took part in raids against the Mersserschmitt factory in Augsburg, oil refineries at Brux and marshalling yards at Keil.

Swanton Morley
Opened in September 1940 for 105 Squadron with Blenheim IVs. These aircraft carried out day and night bombing raids on coastal patrols. Later, 226 Squadron moved in flying Boston IIIs. Several other units shared this base throughout the war including No. 1508 BAT Flight, No. 1515 Blind Approach Training Flight and 1482 B & G Flights flying Venturas, Mitchells and Martinets.

Swannington
85 and 157 Squadrons arrived at Swannington during the spring of 1944 flying Mosquitoes armed with A1 Mk X radar. They acted as bomber support units, playing an important part in tracking down and destroying low-flying V-rockets.

Thorpe Abbots
Opened during the spring of 1943 with the arrival of the American 100th Bomb Group. Listed as the Group suffering the greatest losses during the war, it was known as 'the Bloody Hundredth' and flew missions over France and Germany. The 100th was awarded three special Distinguished Unit citations. The RAF took over the station in 1945.

Tibenham
B-24s of the 44th Bomb group were among the first to operate from this base in late 1943. They flew 282 missions against targets in Munich, Duneberg and Ludwigshaven and took part in softening up raids on pre-invasion targets.

Watton
Opened in 1939 to Blenheims of 34 Squadron, closely followed by 21 Squadron. A busy field during the war, used by B-17s, B-24s and Mosquitoes. Watton also served as an advanced training school for pilots. The Americans took over in 1943, and handed it back to the RAF in 1945.

Wendling
The American 392nd moved in during 1943 as part of the 8th Air Force flying B-24Hs. Targets included the Gotha factory, steel works at Brunswick and strafing raids during the Rhine crossing. Taken over by the RAF in 1945.

West Raynham
Opened in 1939 with Blenheims of 101 Squadron. Used at first as a training station, then fully operational in 1940 for units such as 18 Squadron, 114 Blenheim Squadron, 614 and 180 Squadrons.

Weybourne
Used during the 1930s to launch radio-controlled Queen Bee targets for gunnery practice. In 1941, T Flight, 1 AACU was formed to carry out target practice using rockets. Aircraft stopped using this base in 1942.

CAMBRIDGE

Alconbury
Opened in 1938 when 63 Squadron took over. During the Battle of Britain, Alconbury was to play an active role hosting VX Squadron. Later, Wellington IIs flew from here. In August 1942, the Americans moved in with B-24 Liberators. A year later the 482nd Bomb group, flying B-17s arrived to carry out extensive raids on German factories. Radar bombing equipment was tested at Alconbury. The Americans left in June 1945.

Bassingbourn
Opened in 1938. Wellingtons of 215 Squadron moved in soon after the outbreak of war in September 1939. Ansons were here in 1940, joined later by Whitleys of 10 and 78 Squadrons on Mediterranean missions. The Americans arrived in 1942 with B-17s of the 91st Bomb Group. Handed back to the RAF in 1945.

Bottisham
Tiger Moths arrived in 1940, armed and ready for the expected invasion of East Anglia. In 1942, 241 Squadron Mustangs arrived. The American 361st Fighter Group flying P-47s arrived in 1943. They carried out strafing raids.

Bourn
Wellingtons and Stirlings were here in 1941, with Wellington IIIs of 101 Squadron moving in during the winter of 1942, 97 Squadron Lancasters in 1943 and Mosquito XXs from 162 Squadron in 1944.

Cambridge
Famous for its flight of Tiger Moths. Under fire several times during the war. Damaged planes were repaired by Marshalls, a famous local firm.

Castle Camps
85 Squadron and 73 Squadron moved into this fighter base in 1940. Mosquitoes were tested here in 1942 and 151 and 25 Squadrons moved in later in the war.

Caxton Gibbett
Opened in 1940 as a landing ground for Tiger Moths. Suffered bombing and strafing raids during the war.

Duxford
Dating back to 1919, this important field saw a variety of aircraft between the wars. Soon after the outbreak of war, Blenheim 1Fs of 222 Squadron moved in. Other Squadrons based at Duxford were 264, 19 and 66, important in the Dunkirk crisis and the Battle of Britain. The Americans arrived in 1943.

Fowlmere
Opened in June 1940 for 19 Squadron flying Sptifires. Later the Eagle Squadron flying Hurricanes moved in. By 1941, Spitfire IIs of 54 Squadron had arrived at Fowlmere. The American 339th Fighter Group flying P-51Bs also used this base.

Glatton
Used by the 457th Bomb Group flying B-17Gs against enemy airfields and other vital targets.

Gransden
Wellingtons of 192 Squadron flew from here in 1942. Gransden is best remembered for experimental radar and Pathfinder Navigational Training Units, working in close conjunction with Canadian personnel.

Graveley
Used by 161 (Special Duties) Squadron and 35 Squadron flying Halifax IIs.

Lord's Bridge
Used mainly as a relief landing ground, mainly by groups of trainee pilots flying Tiger Moths.

Mepal
Completed in 1943, this airfield was originally built as a sub-station housing Stirling bombers. No.s 7 and 49 Squadrons were among the last to leave at the end of the war.

Oakington
Opened in July 1940 when 218 Squadron with Blenheim IVs moved in. Later that year, No. 3 Photographic Reconnaissance Unit arrived. No. 7 Squadron flying Stirling bombers was based here.

Snailwell
Opened March 1941 for Lysanders of 268 Squadron. A year later, Typhoons, closely followed by the American 347th Squadron flying P-39 Aircobras moved in. 1426 Enemy Aircraft Flight, flying captured Luftwaffe aircraft in undercover operations over enemy-held territory also operated from Snailwell. Closed at the end of the war.

Somersham
Used for top secret missions flown under cover of darkness. Little is known about the nature of these missions – but local rumour says that even after the war, there was night-time activity at Somersham.

Steeple Morden
Another mystery field, where Wellington bombers could be seen. In 1942, the Americans moved in with the 3rd US Photo Group and later the 355th Fighter Group flying P-47s.

Upwood
A pre-war station opened in 1937 for 63 Squadron and its flight of Fairey Battles. In 1940, Upwood was used as a Blenheim training school, while in 1943, extensive changes were made to the runway for Lancaster and Halifax bombers. Towards the end of the war, 139 Squadron was flying Mosquito XXs on night missions.

Wratting Common
Originally known as West Wickham, this airfield was opened for operational flying in May 1943 with the arrival of 90 Squadron, flying Stirling bombers. Three months later, the base became Wratting Common. Later, 1651 Conversion Unit moved in with Stirlings. The last Squadron to use Wratting Common was the 195th, operating Lancasters.

Warboys
In 1942, 156 Squadron moved in with Wellingtons. By 1943, 1507 BAT flight had also arrived. Lancasters and Mosquitoes of Pathfinder Force Navigational Training Units were here in 1944.

Waterbeach
Wellington bombers of 99 Squadron were first to use this field in 1941, followed by 1651 Conversion Unit in 1942. Later in 1943, 514 Squadron arrived flying Lancaster IIs.

Witchford
Situated on the Isle of Ely, this airfield opened in 1943 with Wellington bombers of 196 Squadron. Later, 115 Squadron with Lancasters flew from here against enemy targets. Closed in 1945.

Wyton
Opened during the first world war as a training school for the RFC, this important field was to witness a lot of pre-war activity. 40 Squadron operated from Wyton during the war and suffered severe losses. The base is still in use today.

THE ESSEX REGIMENT

1st Battalion (Regular)
This battalion was serving in Egypt and Cyprus when war broke out. Moved to the Sudan and took part in the Abyssinian campaign. They were at the siege of Tobruk, then on to Assam and Burma where they formed two Chindit columns, the 44th and 56th. One of the last units to leave India.

2nd Battalion (Regular)
Stationed at regimental HQ, Warley Barracks, Essex and mobilised on August 24, 1939. Deployed in detachments between Purfleet, Brentford and Finchley. On September 1, concentrated at Warley, crossing to France on September 16. Returned via Dunkirk on May 30. Remained on Home Defence duties, mainly on the south coast, until returning to France with the Normandy landing on D-Day. Fought through to Germany – and served in Clacton from February to March 1944.

1/4th Battalion (original TA unit)
Based around Ilford, mobilised to defend airfields around Epping (North Weald and Hornchurch). Moved to Witham/Kelvedon in November 1939, and on to Northumberland in 1940. Moved to North Africa via Sierra Leone in August 1940 and to the western desert, visiting Egypt, Palestine and Cyprus on the way. In April 1941, they fought at El Alamein and at Mareth. The Battalion took a heavy battering at the battle for Monte Cassino, serving as part of the 4th Indian Division, crossing later to Greece where they were witness to the political troubles of the time.

2/4th Battalion (duplicate TA unit)
Formed on the 'doubling-up' of the TA. Did not go to war but trained drafts

at home. Served in Suffolk, defending Leiston and Aldeburgh from November 1939 to April 1940. Moved to Northumberland. Returned to Aldeburgh in November 1941. Served in Berkshire, Kent, Yorkshire and Hampshire until August 1944, when it moved to Southwold, then on to Shorncliffe in November 1944. Moved to Aylsham in 1945 where it was placed in suspended animation.

1/5th Battalion (original TA unit)
Based in Chelmsford, the 5th Bn. divided in June 1939 into the 1/5th (West) and 2/5th (East) battalions. It was mobilised on September 1, 1939 to guard locations around Essex and was concentrated in Chelmsford in October 1939. It provided parties of men to work on east coast defences, leaving for Northumberland in April 1940. In December it moved to Kent from where it left for the Middle East via Gourock and Durban. After garrison duty in Egypt, Syria and Iraq, the Battalion crossed to Taranto in Italy in September 1943, taking part in the assault crossings of the rivers Trigno, Sangro, Arielli and the Battle of Villa Grande. In July 1944, a move was made to Egypt, and in February 1945 to north west Europe where the Battalion took part in the advance into Germany and the crossing of the Elbe. The unit was finally placed in suspended animation in June 1946.

2/5th Battalion
Formed as the duplicate unit of the original 5th Battalion, the 2/5th (East) was mobilised at the same time and deployed defending Harwich – the same task that the 5th had performed in 1914. In March 1940, the unit was concentrated at Colchester, moving to Northumberland in April. On December 17, the unit sailed for an unknown destination, which turned out to be Freetown, Sierra Leone, where many of the men were struck down by malaria. In July 1941, the Battalion reached Egypt which they left in October for Iraq. In June 1942, they moved to a position in Deir-el-Shein in front of El Alamein. As part of the 18th Indian Brigade Group they were left to hold a rocky position, unsupported by tanks or artillery. When the 15th Panzer Division appeared out of the desert, the unit was completely overrun and the vast majority of men taken prisoner. The CO was exonerated of blame in a susequent enquiry.

6th Battalion TA
Converted in 1939 to a searchlight unit, it formed two units on doubling the 1/6th Bn. (64 Searchlight Regiment) and 2/6th (65 Searchlight Regiment). In 1940, the two units joined the Royal Artillery. They served in Norfolk, Yorkshire and Northamptonshire. The 2/6th also served in Belgium.

7th Battalion TA
Converted into anti-aircraft artillery in 1935, forming the 29th (The Essex Regiment) Heavy Anti-Aircraft Regiment. Served in the Thames estuary, the Clyde, Newcastle, Kent, Plymouth and Bristol. Sailed for North Africa on December 11, 1942 and served in Italy from November 1943.

8th Battalion
A wartime unit formed on July 4, 1940. Served at Redditch and Sherborne, the latter on anti-invasion duties. Converted to 153 Regiment, RAC (The Essex Regiment) in November 1931, they sailed for Normandy on D-Day plus 28. After 12 days of battle, and having lost 18 Churchill tanks, the unit was disbanded as being the junior of the 34th Army Tank Brigade. One squadron was detached and formed C (Essex) Squadron of 107 Regiment (The King's Own) RAC, serving right through to the end of the war, latterly as bodyguard to Montgomery.

9th Battalion
Formed July 10, 1940. Served also in the West Midlands, Dorset and Devon. In November 1942, the unit was converted to the 11th (Essex) Medium Regiment RA. The Regiment landed in Normandy on July 14, 1944, and saw action around Boulogne, Calais, Cap Gris Nez, Flushing and Walchenen. They also supported the crossing of the Rhine.

10th Battalion
Again formed in July 1940, they served at Dovercourt from October, working on the defences of Harwich, both seaward and landward during the winter. In May 1941, the unit moved inland to defend airfields and in January 1942, to Harlow and Much Hadham. In 1942, they moved to Woodbridge for three months of coastal defence work. In February 1943, the unit was converted to the 9th (Home Counties) Bn. Parachute Regiment. The Regiment parachuted into France on D-Day to destroy the Merville Battery. The 1939–45 Roll of Honour lists 1594 names.

THE SUFFOLK REGIMENT

In 1939, the Suffolk Regiment consisted of two (1st and 2nd) serving Battalions, with one Suffolk Territorial Battalion (the 4th) and the 1st Battalion , Cambridgeshire Regiment, forming part of the same corps.

Regimental HQ was established at Bury St Edmunds with the chapel in the Church of St Mary's.

On the outbreak of war, the 1st Battalion returned from Malta to Gibraltar barracks, undertaking an extensive recruitment and training programme. In October 1939, they were shipped to France for emergency digging-in near Metz. Actively involved in the massive withdrawal through Belgium and France, the 1st Suffolks took part in the unfortunate attack at Watrelos on the Franco-Belgian border, meeting with considerable opposition resulting in the withdrawal of the Battalion with 75 casualties.

Remnants of the Battalion eventually reached Dunkirk sailing aboard the *Ben Macree* to safety.

During the spring of 1939, another TA unit was formed – the 5th Battalion with over 6200 men joining the colours in just two months. For two years they served with the Home Defence Force, but on October 29, 1941, they sailed for Singapore and were subsequently captured by the Japanese.

The 7th Suffolk fought in North Africa, becoming part of the 142nd Regiment, RAC, then on to Europe before being disbanded in October 1944.

The 1st Battalion was eventually made up to strength after Dunkirk, but for the best part of three years, saw service in Britain.

They took part in the D-Day landings on Queen beach, campaigning through to Germany.

The 2nd Battalion served mainly in India and were in the push against Japanese forces.

ROYAL NORFOLK REGIMENT

The Royal Norfolk Regiment had Battalions at various locations in 1939. Regimental HQ was Britannia Barracks, Norwich. Some of the Battalions were in East Anglia during the war for regrouping, defence and training. The Regiment is credited with five VCs for action in various campaigns from 1939–45.

1st Battalion
India, England, France, Holland and Germany.

2nd Battalion
France (BEF), England, India and Burma.

Depot
England

4th Battalion
England, Malaya (Singapore POW).

5th Battalion
England, Malaya (Singapore POW).

6th Battalion
England, Malaya (Singapore POW).

7th Battalion
France (BEF POW), England and France.

8th/30th Battalion
England, Algeria, Sicily, Italy.

70th Battalion
England (Young Soldiers).

Norfolk Home Guard
17 Battalions serving in England.

THE CAMBRIDGESHIRE REGIMENT

This fine old county regiment dates back to the 1860s, and boasts a chequered career, having been amalgamated with several other regiments throughout 80 years of service. They have served alongside the Huntingdonshire, Essex and Suffolk regiments. On the outbreak of war, they became part of the Suffolk Regiment, and were lost at the fall of Singapore.

Members of the Cambridge University Senior Training Corps eventually filtered into OTC units while others joined special Young Soldier battalions of the Home Guard, serving with coastal and inland AA and searchlight batteries around the region.

GERMAN POW CAMPS IN EAST ANGLIA

Camp no 26: Barton Field, Ely, Cambridgeshire.

Camp no 30: Carpenter's Road, Stratford, Essex.

Camp no 45: Trumpington, Cambridgeshire.

Camp no 56: Botesdale, Diss, East Suffolk.

Camp no 78: High Garrett, Braintree, Essex.

Camp no 82: Hampton Green, Fakenham, Norfolk (also at Aldborough, Norfolk).

Camp no 85: Victoria Camp, Brandon Road, Mildenhall, Bury St Edmunds, Suffolk.

Camp no 90: Friday Bridge, Wisbech, Cambridgeshire.

Camp no 116: Mill Lane, Hatfield Heath, Bishop's Stortford, Essex.

Camp no 129: Ashford Lodge, Halstead, Essex.

Camp no 130: West Fen Militia, Ely, Cambridgeshire.

Camp no 131: Uplands Camp, Diss, Norfolk.

Camp no 132: Kimberley Park, Kimberley, Norfolk.

Camp no 171: Bungay Base Camp, Bungay, Suffolk.

Camp no 180: Trumpington, Cambridgeshire,

(also at Saffron Walden, Essex).

Camp nos 186 and 204: Berechurch Hall, Colchester, Essex.

Camp no 231: Redgrave Park, Diss, Norfolk (military hospital).

Camp no 236: White House, Church Hill, Loughton, Essex.

Camp no 253: Mousehold Heath, Norwich

Camp no 255: RAF Camp, Snettisham, King's Lynn, Norfolk.

Camp no 258: RAF Camp, Seething, Brooke, Norfolk.

Camp no 260: Hardwick House, Bury St Edmunds, Suffolk.

Camp no 266: Hutted Camp, Langdon Hills, Laindon, Essex.

Camp no 273: Flixton Airfield, Flixton, Bungay, Suffolk,

(also at Debach Airfield, Debach, Woodbridge, Suffolk).

Camp no 272: RAF Airfield, Attleborough, Norfolk.

Camp no 280: North Lynn Farm, King's Lynn, Norfolk.

Camp no 281: Aldborough, Norfolk.

Camp no 286: Purfleet and Romford, Essex.

Camp no 409: Wolterton Camp, Aylsham, Norfolk.

Camp no 654: No 4 POW Transit Camp, Purfleet, Essex (also Camp 655).

Camp no 670: Shaftesbury Camp, Dovercourt, Harwich, Essex (also Camp 680).

Camp no 740: Harwich Transit Camp, Harwich, Essex.

Camp no 1025: Milton Road, Histon, Cambridgeshire.

An unlisted Group Pioneer Corps HQ was established at Newmarket. In addition to these main camps, it was common practice to farm out groups of POWs with various landowners, who either accomodated them in Nissen huts or took them in to live with the family or farm workers. There are few surviving official records of these special billets.

BRANCHES OF THE SERVICE

ARP: Air Raid Precautions.

AFS: Auxiliary Fire Service.

ATS: Auxiliary Territorial Service (womens).

BRCS: British Red Cross Service.

CD: Civil Defence.

CMP: Corps of Military Police (later Royal Military Police).

CNR: Civil Nursing Reserve.

ENSA: Entertainments National Service Association.

HG: Home Guard.

LDV: Local Defence Volunteers.

NAAFI: Navy, Army and Air Force Institute.

NFS: National Fire Service.

QAIMNS: Queen Alexandra's Imperial Military Nursing Service.

QARNNS: Queen Alexandra's Royal Naval Nursing Service.

RAAF: Royal Australian Air Force.

RA: Royal Artillery.

RAMC: Royal Army Medical Corps.

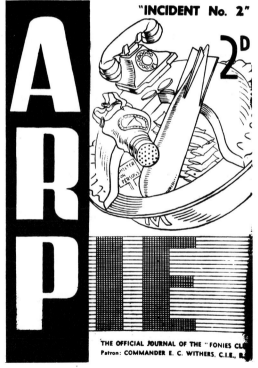

"INCIDENT No. 2"

2D

THE OFFICIAL JOURNAL OF THE "FONIES CL
Patron: COMMANDER E. C. WITHERS, C.I.E., R

WOMEN'S LAND ARMY (ENGLAND AND WALES).
RELEASE CERTIFICATE.

The Women's Land Army for England and Wales acknowledges with appreciation the services given by

MRS. E.M. DIXON, W.L.A. 10080.

who has been an enrolled member for the period from

30th. June 1939 to 19th. November 1945

and has this day been granted a willing release.

Date 19th. Nov. 1945

COUNTY SECRETARY, WOMEN'S LAND ARMY.

RAOC: Royal Army Ordnance Corps.

RASC: Royal Army Service Corps.

RAVC: Royal Army Veterinary Corps.

RCAF: Royal Canadian Air Force.

RM: Royal Marines.

RNVR: Royal Naval Volunteer Reserve.

RNZAF: Royal New Zealand Air Force.

ROC: Royal Observer Corps.

SPC: Special Police Constable.

WAAF: Women's Auxiliary Air Force.

WLA: Women's Land Army.

WRNS: Women's Royal Naval Service.

WVS: Women's Voluntary Service.

BRITISH MILITARY TERMS

AA: Anti-aircraft.

Ack Ack: Anti-aircraft fire.

AACS: Air & Airways Communications Service.

AACU: Anti-aircraft Co-operation Unit.

A&AEE: Aeroplane and Armaments Experimental Establishment.

A&IEU: Armament and Instrument Experimental Unit.

AAP: Aircraft Acceptance Park.

AAU: Aircraft Assembly Unit.

AATF: Anti-aircraft and Target Flight.

ACHU: Aircrew Holding Unit.

ADGB: Air Defence of Great Britain.

AEF: Air Experience Flight.

AFS: Advanced Flying School.

AFEE: Airborne Forces Experimental Establishment.

AGS: Air Gunnery School.

AI: Airborne Interception (radar set in British aircraft).

AMWD: Air Ministry Works Department.

ANS: Air Navigation School.

AONS: Air Observer Navigation School.

AOC: Air Observer Corps.

APC: Armament Practice Camp.

APS: Armament Practice Station.

ASH: Narrow Beam Radar.

ASR: Air-Sea Rescue.

BAT: Blind Approach Training Flight.

BG: Bombardment Group.

B&G: Bombing and Gunnery Flight.

BLEU: Blind Landing Experimental Unit.

BSDU: Bomber Support Development Unit.

CAACU: Civilian Anti-Aircraft Co-operation Unit.

CAM: Civilian Aircraft Merchant (Ship).

CCRC: Combat Crew Replacement Centre.

CSE: Central Signals Establishment.

DFCS: Day Fighter Combat School.

FAA : Fleet Air Arm.

GRU: General Reconnaissance Unit.

LNSF: Light Night Striking Force (Mosquitoes).

MAEF: Marine Aircraft Experimental Establishment.

MAP: Ministry of Aircraft Production.

OCTU: Officer Cadet Training Unit.

OTU: Operational Training Unit.

PRU: Photographic Reconnaissance Unit.

USAAC: United States Army Air Corps.

USAAF: United States Army Air Force.

W/T: Wireless Telegraphy.

GERMAN MILITARY TERMS

Anzundergruppe: A flying unit charged with lighting fires in a target area for the guidance of other, less well-equipped units. Also known as a Beleuchtergruppe, and later Pfadfindergruppe.

Aufklärungsgruppe: Reconnaissance wing.

AZ: Aufschlag Zünder - impact bomb fuse.

Beobachter: Observer (navigator/bomb aimer).

Blitz: Literally lightning.

Blitzlichteylinderische: Photographic flash bomb.

Bombenmine: 1000kg sea mine adapted to be dropped on land, with or without a parachute, named the Monika or G mine.

Bordfunker: Wireless Operator.

Bordschutze: Air Gunner.

Bordmechaniker: Flight Engineer.

Brandebombe: Incendiary bomb.

El.AZ: Electrische Aufschlag Zünder - electrical impact bomb fuse.

El.Z: Electrische Zünder - electrical bomb fuse.

Erprobungsgruppe 210: Experimental flight development wing equipped with the Bf 110 during the Battle of Britain and the Blitz. Later equipped with the Me 210.

Esau: 1000kg armour-piercing bomb.

Fallschirmleuchtbombe: Parachute flare.

Fieseler Fi 103: V-1 flying bomb.

Fliegerabwehrkanone: AA fire, commonly known as flak.

Flammenbombe: Fire or oil bomb.

Fliegerkorps: A command, subsidiary to a Luftflotte, and responsible for a variable number of Geschwader.

Flugzeugfuhrer: Pilot.

Fritz: 1400 kg armour piercing bomb.

Fuhrungsstab: Operations staff of the Luftwaffe High Command.

Geschwader: Operational unit, approximately equivalent to a Group in the RAF. Normally made up of three operational Gruppen and a Staff Flight, with a total establishment of 100 aircraft. Pre-fixed Kampf (bomber), Jagd (fighter), Zerstorer (long-range fighter) to determine exact role.

Grossbritannien: Great Britain.

Gruppe GR: Operational unit, approximately equivalent to a Wing in the RAF. Normally made up of three Staffeln and a Staff Flight with a total establishment of approximately 30 aircraft. An independent bomber Gruppe was prefixed Kampf.

Gruppen Kommandeur: Commander of a Gruppe or Wing.

He: Ernst Heinkel Flugzuegwerkes GmbH – manufacturer of Heinkel aircraft.

Heer: German army.

Jagdgeschwader: Fighter group.

Ju: Junkers Flugzuegwerke und Motorwerke GmbH –

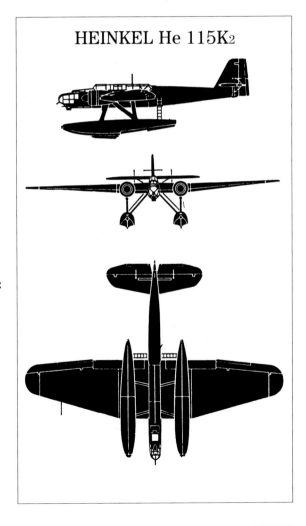

HEINKEL He 115K2

manufacturer of Junkers aircraft.

Kampgeschwader: Bomber Group.

Kampfgruppe: Bomber Wing.

Kette: Flight, usually three bombers or four fighters.

Knickebein: Code name for German navigation beam, literally meaning "crooked leg."

Kopfring: Special steel ring fitted to the nose of a bomb to prevent excessive penetration into the ground.

Kriegsberichter: War correspondent.

Kriegsmarine: Navy.

Splitterbombe (butterfly bomb).

Kustenfliegergruppe: Coastal Reconnaissance Wing.

Leuchtcylinderische: Parachute flare (LC50).

Lehrgeschwader: Instructional/operational development group.

Luftflotte: Air Fleet.

Luftmine: Sea mine adapted to be dropped on land by parachute.

Langzeitzunder: Long time delay bomb fuse.

Max: 2500 kg thin-case general purpose bomb.

Mit Verzogerungszunder: Delayed action bomb fuse.

Nachtjagdgeschwader: Night Fighter Group.

Oberbefehlshaber: Commander-in-Chief.

Oberkommando der Luftwaffe: Air Force High Command.

Ohne Verzögerung: Bomb fuse without time delay.

Panzerbombe Cylinderisch: Armour-piercing bomb.

Phosphorbrandbombe: Phosphorus incendiary bomb.

Reichsluftfahrtministerium: German Air Ministry.

Sprengbombe-Cylindrisch: Thin-cased general purpose bomb.

Sprengbombe-Dickwandig: Thick-cased semi armour piercing fragmentation bomb.

Schleuderstart: Winch-assisted method of take off.

Schwerpunkt: Aiming point for raid.

Seenotflugkommando: Air Sea Rescue Service.

Seeauberangriff: Pirate or tip-and-run attacks.

Splitterbombe: Anti-personnel butterfly bomb.

Sprengbombe: High-explosive bomb.

Sprengbrandbombe: Explosive incendiary bomb.

Stab: Staff.

Staffel: Normally nine aircraft.

Staffelkapitän: Squadron Commander.

Störangriffe: Harassing attack.

St G: Stukgeschwader : Ju 88 flying unit.

Stuka: Ju 87 dive bomber.

Vergeltungswaffe-1: Reprisal weapon. German pilotless aircraft launched against Britain. **Vergeltungswaffe-2** was its successor It was long-range and could fly at high altitude.

Wehrmacht: The German armed forces.

Wettererkundungs: Weather reconnaissance.

X-Gerät: X-equipment installed in aircraft for the reception of X-Verfahren signals.

X-Verfahren: X-system, VHF multi-beam precision bombing system.

Zerstörer: Long-range fighter bomber.

Zerstörziele: Literally "destruction" raids against specific factories.

Zielraum: Target areas.

Zectzünder: Time bomb fuse.

Zunder: Bomb fuse.

ACKNOWLEDGMENTS

My heartfelt thanks to literally dozens of individuals who over the past decade have taken time to answer lengthy questionnaires and endure hours of interviews; without their help this second edition could never have been completed. Although impossible to list everyone concerned, I feel it only fair to thank the editors of numerous magazines and newspapers who afforded me space in their publications. To the research staff of Boulton & Paul, Norwich, Marconi of Chelmsford, Ford of Dagenham (for use of pictures as well as information), and Paxman Diesel of Colchester. To Ian Hook, Essex Regimental Museum and Lt Col H J Orpen-Smellie. Terence C Charman, Imperial War Museum, Victor Gray, County Archivist, Essex Record Office, Nicholas Clough (*Perspective Scientific* for the loan of geiger-counters), Brig H E Kirby, Eunice Wilson (researcher), Sir Geoffrey Tuttle, J A Wheeler, Wing-Commander E F Price, John I Hopkin, R H Bland, D W Orton, G H Osborn, Bill Hawkins, W J Perry, Col H Cramphorn, Karl H Wehn, Harry Whitbread, Edda Schmidt, R A S Pagani, Frank Harwood, H J Ahier, A J Willing, Ron Williams, John Maclaren, Joe Miere, Winfried Lierenfeld, Mr S Bradford, Peter Korner, Percy Darvell (for the loan of the Barnes Wallis, Shingle Street, photograph), Ken Jarmin, B J Proctor, George Coates and C D Robinson. And not forgetting Mr Fred Martin, the late Roger Weeley and late Captain K Seabrooke (all who served with the special secret underground Home Guard army). Mrs G Clutten; the late Hubert Inman and late Lt Commander W A A Greenwell, RNVR, Officer Commanding the network of special Decoy Sites. Group Captain Colin Gray, DFC, DSO, Lt General Avi. Baron M Donnet, CVO, DFC, Mrs Rose Kennedy (USA), Mr R Kennell, and the editors of *Comrade* and *Action*.

Special thanks to my old kamerad and friend Victor S Wilson (for detailed and technical German translations); Bill Gadd, and fellow-author Gordon Kinsey who very kindly shared their accumulated wealth of knowledge and know-how on crashed aircraft sites, little recorded air-raids plus the location of wartime airfields around the region. Last but by no means least, colleague and friend, former BBC producer, Douglas Salmon.

Back cover photograph of author: George Georgiou.
Front cover picture: Cadbury-Schweppes.
Pictures, page 55: Ford. Page 137, Heather Stanway.